Do You Know Who You Are?

Reading the Buddha's Discourses

Krishnan Venkatesh

MERCER UNIVERSITY PRESS | *Macon, Georgia*
2018

MUP/ P573

© 2018 by Mercer University Press
Published by Mercer University Press
1501 Mercer University Drive
Macon, Georgia 31207
All rights reserved

9 8 7 6 5 4 3 2 1

Books published by Mercer University Press are printed on acid-
free paper that meets the requirements of the American National
Standard for Information Sciences—Permanence of Paper for
Printed Library Materials.

Printed and bound in the United States.

This book is set in Adobe Caslon

ISBN   978-0-88146-679-9
Cataloging-in-Publication Data is available from the Library of Congress

Do You Know Who You Are?

Reading the Buddha's Discourses

For Jet Anton,
who was conceived at the same time as this book
and who is by far the superior work

Contents

Acknowledgments

I would like to give special thanks to two Buddhist websites for their kindness and generosity in promulgating excellent translations of the Pali Discourses and in making them freely available to quote and excerpt. *Access to Insight* contains several translations of most of the Discourses, as well as a vast body of commentary and instruction; *SuttaCentral* has all the Discourses in Pali as well as many modern languages. Besides studying the suttas specifically chosen for this volume, I have learned a lot from reading widely on both sites.

In addition I have benefited deeply from two decades of conversation on these texts in the Eastern Classics program at St. John's College, Santa Fe. To my students and colleagues I am grateful for many honest and original insights—in particular, Claudia Hauer, Patricia Greer, and Shelley Mason.

Finally, I would like to thank my publisher at Mercer, Marc Jolley, for understanding and believing in this project of seeking out living wisdom from these ancient words.

Atta (Pali), *Atman* (Sanskrit): the "self" or soul, the essence of a being.

Bhikkhu: a mendicant monk, *or* someone who has renounced everything to follow the Buddha's teachings.

Brahmin: highest of the four castes in Hindu society, the caste of priests and scholars.

Citta: mind, state of mind, or mental processes.

Dhamma (Pali), *Dharma (*Sanskrit)*:* the essential order of the world, the Buddha's teachings (which express that order), phenomena.

Digha Nikaya: Collection of Longer Discourses.

Dukkha: suffering, unhappiness, dissatisfaction.

Jhana: higher mental state resulting from meditation and concentration.

Khandas (Pali), *skandhas* (Sanskrit): the aggregates, or "heaps" of the five fundamental constituents of all sentient beings: body, sensation or feeling (see *vedana*), perception, volition, consciousness.

Majjhima Nikaya: Collection of Middle-Length Discourses.

Nibbana (Pali), *Nirvana* (Sanskrit): literally "burning out," "blowing out," or extinguishing; final release from the round of suffering.

Nikaya: volume or collection.

Pali: one of the many vernacular languages of South Asia in which the Discourses were written.

Samyutta Nikaya: Collection of Grouped or Connected Discourses.

Sutta (Pali), *Sutra* (Sanskrit): in Buddhism, a canonical text or scripture. Literally, a "thread."

Tanha: literally, "thirst;" usually translated "craving."

Tathagatha: literally "thus come one" or "thus gone one," the word the Buddha uses when referring to himself.

Upadana: literally, "fuel;" usually translated "attachment" or "clinging."

Vedana: the pleasant, unpleasant, or neutral feelings arising from contact with sense objects.

Vinaya: "leading out," "education," "discipline;" the system of rules for monastic life.

Essaying the Buddha:
An Introduction

In the West, the most powerful challenges to established traditions and systems of thought come in the reported utterances of two men who were killed by their societies: Socrates and Jesus. The former created "philosophy" by teaching us to ask questions about the assumptions that underpin all our opinions, and woke us up to our ignorance about everything; the latter shook us into a higher way of being founded on the mystery of love, threatening social stability by exposing the mechanisms of blame and violent sacrifice on which societies are built. In the East—expanding from India and Nepal to the Greek kingdoms of present-day Afghanistan and thence through China to all of East Asia—it was the Buddha who gave the comparable challenge, and it was a challenge even more radical than any the world had ever seen.

Put simply, the Buddha summons us to *look* at ourselves and see directly, *for ourselves*, what is there. It is a more radical challenge than even Socrates' or Jesus', because it asks us to sit with ourselves and watch activity such as thinking and loving as they are taking place. Only through this empirical practice will we learn the truth about ourselves and our lives. What emerges from this observation, the practice of mindfulness, is the foundation of the Buddha's teaching—but this teaching can make no sense if we do not do the practice. In this book I assume that most thoughtful people already do *some* of the practice of empirical introspection, and that much of the Buddha's teaching makes sense if we stop to scrutinize our experience. The Discourses are a manual for self-scrutiny, a curriculum of exercises through which we learn how to encounter ourselves for the first time.

The Texts

Thus I have heard. This, the characteristic opening sentence of the Pali discourses of the Buddha, makes us aware at the outset that what we are about to get is words refracted through memory, or through the memory of a memory. What relation do these words have to the earliest, most authentic words of the historical Gotama Buddha? No one can know the answer to this, but the teachings of the Discourses have such power, originality, and cogency that it is hard to resist viewing them as issuing authentically from a single, profound intelligence. The historical Gotama comes to us deflected by memory and the creative imagination, like the historical Jesus and the historical Socrates, but the deflected images taken in themselves yield such rich insight that their historical origins—which are not directly accessible to us anyway—are of only secondary interest to the reader who wants to understand the insight. It doesn't bother me at all that I can only fantasize about the historical Socrates on the basis of the Socrates of Plato and the Socrates of Xenophon, who bear only a tenuous resemblance to one another both in the kinds of things they say and in how they say it.

Thus I have heard: About two and a half thousand years ago a single human being discovered a way to reconceive the problem of unhappiness. Realizing that all the various paths hitherto proposed as paths out of suffering were really either dead ends or paths that led deeper into suffering, Gotama Buddha—as the legend goes—sat under a tree and wouldn't budge until he had understood the reasons for suffering and found a true path out of it. He knew that his discovery would be opposed and misunderstood by all the orthodoxies of his day, but despite his reluctance, he was persuaded to teach, and over the rest of his life held a vast number of conversations with many different kinds of people. Some of these people were perplexed by him, but most of them, after hearing what he had to say, could simply not go back to the way they had been living. After his death these conversations were recollected, and then collected, by his disciples; indeed, the Canon is mainly attributed to the prodigious memory of his closest disciple and attendant, Ananda. It was only in 29 BCE, about 450 years after the Buddha's death, that the conversations were written down and became the Pali Canon, which comprises thousands of pages of the Buddha's remembered discourses.

Their style is terse, formulaic, methodical, and unappealing, full of repetition and patterned phrasing designed for efficient memorization. I've observed a number of different charismatic spiritual teachers and know that somebody who attracted as many devoted followers as the Buddha did could not have spoken in such a stern, charmless manner. It is as if his lovable, living speech has been freeze-dried and preserved in tight foil packets for future use. The writers have meticulously shunned any possibility of verbal seduction by stylistic beauty, and are forcing us to relate only to what the words are saying. While the first impression made by the Suttas is of a forbidding and desiccated austerity, after some exposure their atmosphere starts to feel like the healthy, refreshing dryness of mountain air: up here we can see farther and smell things more clearly. The studied inelegance of the language slowly acquires the homely, unpretentious beauty of unvarnished wood beams and bare earth floors.

The Canon is vast and daunting: where to begin, and how to proceed? Many students start with the volume called *Majjhima Nikaya*, or the Middle-Length Discourses, which covers the full range of the Buddha's teachings. But this one volume contains 152 dense Suttas and is longer than *War and Peace*. The best way is just to start reading, and if a passage catches your at-

tention, trust that there is a reason for that and dwell on it—
asking exactly what the Buddha is saying, how it is responding to
this particular interlocutor, and what the Buddha is not saying in
this conversation. We can learn from the interlocutor too: what
is his question, and why is it a question for him? Has the Buddha
tailored his response to the character, background, and intelligence of the interlocutor? The dramatic situations of many of the
discourses are themselves integral to the teachings. Reading the
Suttas with careful, thoughtful openness is itself a form of contemplation, training attentiveness to the connections between
thoughts and also developing a habit of testing thoughts against
experience. The Buddha never asks us simply to believe him;
instead, he asks us to "know for ourselves," to penetrate and
comprehend our own experience and everything that is given to
us to experience. The concision and lean abstraction of these
Suttas invite us to enter into them, open them up, and breathe
our own understanding into them: we have to get them to speak
to us by engaging them personally.

The essays in these pages will be *essais* in the classical sense:
attempts, forays, investigations, a daring of myself on the difficult terrain of the text. I try to read the Suttas with my own
mind, paying attention to what the Buddha is actually saying,
and ignoring later interpretations by the various schools and traditions of Buddhism. I read as a non-Buddhist and write for
non-Buddhists—or for Buddhists who are not primarily interested in being Buddhists—hoping that my honest encounter with
the discourses may generate fresh understanding or at least give a
fresh view of old understandings. I read as a struggling, often
dimwitted human being who has found the discourses helpful
and illuminating, and who is plainly incompetent to give any
authoritative overview of the multifarious beast called "Buddhism." Here there will be no descriptions of higher spiritual
states and no speculations about what enlightenment might be

like. My investigation takes place at the lower reaches of the practice, where we learn to understand the human condition, the causes of happiness and unhappiness, how the heart and mind work. It is an immensely satisfying endeavor that can be undertaken wherever we are, at any time, because the conditions for it are universal and omnipresent.

A Plea for Reading

Living in an age that is predominantly materialistic, utilitarian, and anti-intellectual, we will tend to avoid the work of careful, patient thinking that these texts require. If we cannot read a text quickly, we will prefer summaries or clear expositions by an expert. Yet thoughtful people do want to know, What did the Buddha actually say?—because they don't want to be ruled by somebody else's interpretation, and don't just want to be *told*. Fortunately, the Discourses do exist, and even though they are edited and filtered versions of the Buddha, they are nonetheless rich, powerful texts that are the closest that we get to him. Why not just read them, dwell on them, give them the attention that they demand?—in other words, make ourselves vulnerable to them, and let *the texts* read *us*?

"Oh, but we can't understand them without a master," someone will say—usually someone with a spiritual teacher or a member of an established Buddhist school. Perhaps it is true that we cannot understand them fully without help, but that would be true of anything. We can surely understand enough for the text to be of immense value to us. I am not "master" of my car such that I can dismantle and reassemble it, or give an account of how it works, but I can still find it valuable to study the manual. Another typical objection—usually from Buddhist practitioners—goes, "Oh, but reading is not the same as enlightenment!"—and nobody has ever claimed that it was. But if all action comes from thought, and if reading *with intelligence* has an effect on our thoughts, then why would reading not have an effect on actions that might lead to enlightenment?

We have the gift of these volumes of words, and I hope to show in these essays that the words carry insight and depth if we pay attention to each one of them. Brief summaries will not do justice to the electrifying power of the Discourses. Throughout, I will let the Buddha's words stand in the foreground, as I try to articulate the sense that they make to me and that they have brought to my own life.

Part 1

Talking to the Buddha

In the first four of these essays, we will see the Buddha's response to some relatively mundane preoccupations. When speaking to ordinary people and Hindu practitioners, he rarely goes into the core of his teachings, but addresses his interlocutors on their own terms. It was in discourses like these that I first grew to respect the tact, gentleness, and wisdom of this teacher, who always knows what to say and what not to say, who demonstrates reasonableness and moderation in every sentence and none of the relentless one-sidedness of an ideologue. The result of his approach is either to deepen the way his interlocutors already think, or to give them a gentle shaking up. The first of these discourses culminates in the unavoidable question, Do you know who you are?

1. The Buddha Talks to a White Supremacist

Well, not quite. But in the "Assalayana Sutta" (*Majjhima Nikaya*, 93[1]), he does have a detailed conversation with a Brahmin supremacist, and many of his arguments—*mutatis mutandis*—apply to the comparable imbecilities of today's white supremacy movement. While today's Aryan cult is a distinctive and complex mix of vestigial anger from Civil War defeat, identification with German Nazis, despair and rage from economic failures, educational neglect, fundamentalist religion, 19th century collectivism, and nihilist philosophy—among many other things—the Buddha's conversation with the proud young Brahmin Assalayana offers some ways to begin addressing obdurate belief in superiority of caste, race, or any other birth group. A Brahmin supremacist is after all one type of white supremacist, and his belief in supremacy rests on many of the same conceptions.

Assalayana has been sent to dispute the Buddha's claim that the Dhamma is for everybody. As a Brahmin himself, he has been raised to believe that his scholar-priest caste is naturally superior to the other three castes of Hindu society: the warriors, merchants, and workers.

> "Master Gotama, the brahmins say, 'Brahmins are the superior caste; any other caste is inferior. Only brahmins are the fair caste; any other caste is dark. Only brahmins are pure, not non-brahmins. Only brahmins are the sons and offspring of Brahma: born of his mouth, born of Brahma, created by Brahma, heirs of Brahma.' What does Master

[1] Thanissaro Bhikkhu (trans.), "Assalayana Sutta: With Assalayana," (*Majjhima Nikaya* 93), *Access to Insight*, 2010. http://www. accesstoinsight.org/tipitaka/mn/mn.093.than.html.

Gotama have to say with regard to that?"

The Buddha responds first with an observation that we all enter the world through the same anatomical channels:

> "But, Assalayana, the brahmins' brahmin-women are plainly seen having their periods, becoming pregnant, giving birth, and nursing [their children]. And yet the brahmins, being born through the birth canal, say, 'Brahmins are the superior caste...'"

This starting point grounds the discussion in earthy realities that can be perceived clearly by the senses. In this respect no one can be crazy enough to argue that people are fundamentally different. Besides, how delightful it is that a creature who emerges into life from the nether end of its mother can entertain fantasies about its own transcendent superiority!

The Buddha then proceeds Socratically, with questions that he knows Assalayana—being intelligent—will answer in only one way. His next line of attack is based on ethical excellence:

> "What do you think, Assalayana? Is it only a noble warrior who — taking life, stealing, engaging in sexual misconduct, telling lies, speaking divisively, speaking harshly, engaging in idle chatter, greedy, bearing thoughts of ill will, and holding wrong views — on the break-up of the body, after death, reappears in the plane of deprivation, the bad destination, the lower realms, in hell, and not a brahmin? Is it only a merchant...? Is it only a worker who — taking life, stealing, engaging in sexual misconduct, telling lies, speaking divisively, speaking harshly, engaging in idle chatter, greedy, bearing thoughts of ill will, and holding wrong views — on the break-up of the body, after death, reappears in the plane of deprivation, the bad destination, the lower realms, in hell, and not a brahmin?"

> "No, Master Gotama. Even a noble warrior ... Even a

brahmin... Even a merchant... Even a worker... (Members of) all four castes — if they take life, steal, engage in sexual misconduct, tell lies, speak divisively, speak harshly, engage in idle chatter, are greedy, bear thoughts of ill will, and hold wrong views — on the break-up of the body, after death, reappear in the plane of deprivation, the bad destination, the lower realms, in hell."

The reverse applies to Brahmins, warriors, merchants, workers who do good things. Good people are good people, and bad people are bad people, no matter what they come from, and all can expect to suffer the appropriate consequences of their deeds. And even a Brahmin supremacist has to admit to knowing some Brahmins who are terrible people and some farm laborers who are wise and noble.

Next the Buddha asks whether Brahmins, warriors, merchants, and workers have the same relationship to their bodies and to the physical world:

"What do you think, Assalayana? Is it only a brahmin who is capable of taking a loofah and bath powder, going to a river, and scrubbing off dust and dirt, and not a noble warrior, not a merchant, not a worker?"

"What do you think, Assalayana? There is the case where a consecrated noble warrior king might call together one hundred men of different births (and say to them), 'Come, masters. Those of you there born from a noble warrior clan, from a brahmin clan, or from a royal clan: taking an upper fire-stick of saala wood, salala wood, sandalwood, or padumaka wood, produce fire and make heat appear. And come, masters. Those of you there born from an outcast clan, a trapper clan, a wicker workers' clan, a cartwrights' clan, or a scavengers' clan: taking an upper fire-stick from a dog's drinking trough, from a pig's trough, from a dustbin, or of castor-oil wood, produce fire and make heat appear.'

What do you think, Assalayana? Would the fire made by those born from a noble warrior clan, a brahmin clan, or a royal clan — who had produced fire and made heat appear by taking an upper fire-stick of saala wood, salala wood, sandalwood, or padumaka wood — be the only one with flame, color, and radiance, able to do whatever a fire might be needed to do? And would the fire made by those born those born from an outcast clan, a trapper clan, a wicker workers' clan, a cartwrights' clan, or a scavengers' clan — who had produced fire and made heat appear by taking an upper fire-stick from a dog's drinking trough, from a pig's trough, from a dustbin, or of castor-oil wood — be without flame, color, and radiance, unable to do what a fire might be needed to do?"

Using the same materials and techniques, every human being will produce the same fire; thus notions of caste superiority have no basis whatsoever in physical nature.

At this point, in case Assalayana doesn't believe that the laws of physics, chemistry, and biology have any bearing on the issue of ethical supremacy, the Buddha swerves back to the question of merit within the same caste:

"What do you think, Assalayana? There is the case where there might be two brahmin-student brothers, born of the same mother: one learned and initiated, the other not learned and uninitiated. Which of the two would the brahmins serve first at a funeral feast, a milk-rice offering, a sacrifice, or a feast for guests?"

That is, when our comparison is made only between Brahmins, it is clear that merit has nothing to do with birth; at least, we behave as if the more virtuous brother has earned more respect.

On considering this, the *brahmin student Assalayana sat silent, abashed, his shoulders drooping, his head down, brooding, at a*

11

loss for words. He is too intelligent not to see that the supremacist posture is an embarrassment to the intelligence. The Buddha then delivers the *coup de grâce* by retelling the legend of Devala the Dark's confrontation with seven arrogant Brahmins:

> "'But do you know, masters, if the mother who bore you went only with a brahmin, and not with a non-brahmin?'
> "'No, master.'
> "'And do you know if the mothers of the mother who bore you — back seven generations of mothers — went only with brahmins, and not with non-brahmins?'
> "'No, master.'
> "'And do you know if the father who sired you went only with a brahmin woman, and not with a non-brahmin woman?'
> "'No, master.'
> "'And do you know if the fathers of the father who bore you — back seven generations of fathers — went only with brahmin women, and not with non-brahmin women?'
> "'No, master.'"

We know next to nothing about the sexual behavior of our parents, let alone our remote forebears; about some things there is just no knowing. This is analogous to challenging a contemporary white supremacist to take a DNA test—which many will refuse to do or out of bravado agree to tremblingly, because in their heart of hearts they know that they do not really *know* where they come from.

> "'That being the case, do you know who you are?'
> "'That being the case, master, we don't know who we are.'

The Socratic conversation thus leads to a satisfyingly Socratic challenge. How then do we find out who we are?

2. How to Live a Good Human Life:
The Buddha's Advice to Sigala

"Do I have to give up chocolate?" In any serious discussion of the Buddha's Discourses among people who are not Buddhists, there will always be one person who will get annoyed, even outraged, by the idea that the elimination of craving might be the first crucial step in the removal of the conditions for suffering: *Must I do without all my pleasures, like chocolate—or movies—or sexual relationships?* At first it can seem that the Buddha is confronting us with the necessity of getting rid of all the things that make us happy, and that instead of giving us a way out of suffering he would be causing much more of it. This is a perfectly reasonable reaction.

The Buddha never asks a layperson, new to Buddhism, to give up their attachments—because how would they understand the reasons for doing so if the attachments seem good to them right now? To request them to do so would only make them angry and make them more stubborn in their attachment. Most of the Discourses are with disciples, who have already been converted: with them, the Buddha can dig deep into craving and attachment, and not spare their feelings. Even when he is talking with Brahmin ascetics he can refer more freely to the discipline of renunciation, which they are used to. When he is talking with a layperson, however, he doesn't go directly to dependent origination, not-self, or the aggregates, because it wouldn't be constructive or compassionate to do so. How then would he speak to the concerns of someone like me, a person interested in living well but unable yet to fathom the deep meaning of suffering itself, let alone the extinction of it?

In the *Digha Nikaya*, the collection of longer discourses, we meet a young scion of the royal family:

> This is what I heard. On one occasion, the Buddha was living near the town of Rajagaha at a spot in the Bamboo Grove called the Squirrel's Feeding Place.
>
> At that time a young householder named Sigalaka arose early and set out from Rajagaha with freshly washed clothes and hair. With palms together held up in reverence, he was paying respect towards the six directions: that is east, south, west, north, lower and upper. Meanwhile the Buddha dressed himself in the early morning, took his bowl and robe and went in to Rajagaha on alms round. On the way, he saw Sigalaka worshipping the six directions. Seeing this, the Buddha said to him: "Young man, why have you risen in the early morning and set out from Rajagaha to worship in such a way?"
>
> "Dear sir, my father on his deathbed urged me, 'My son, you must worship the directions'. So, dear sir, realizing, honoring, respecting, and holding sacred my father's request, I have risen in the early morning and set out from Rajagaha to worship in this way."
>
> "But, young man, that is not how the six directions should be worshipped according to the discipline of the noble ones." [1]

In a body of work that eschews literary devices and formal elegance, the "meanwhile" is noteworthy: at the same time as Sigalaka is doing x, the Buddha is doing y. Usually the Suttas begin with the Buddha, but this one pointedly begins with his

---

[1] John Kelly, Sue Sawyer, and Victoria Yareham (trans.), "Sigalovada Sutta: The Buddha's Advice to Sigalaka," (*Digha Nikaya* 31), *Access to Insight*, 2005. www.accesstoinsight.org/tipitaka/dn/dn.31.0.ksw0.html.

interlocutor, who is from the beginning placed in the foreground—as if to indicate from the start that the Buddha will enter into his life but not take it over. This Sigalaka is clearly a dutiful son who takes his deceased father's wishes seriously. I imagine this scene taking place just before dawn, before most people are up. Sigalaka has already prepared himself for his devotions "with freshly washed clothes and hair." The Buddha watches, notices the young man's punctilious energy and reverence, gently questions him, and offers instruction. He does not tell him he is wrong, or try to convert him by teaching philosophical profundities; indeed, no attempt is made to change his view of things. After reviewing the usual basic moral precepts, the Buddha gives him a way to deepen the "worship of the six directions." Now this is not a new approach: even in the Upanishads the six directions are interpreted allegorically, because "worship" of them cannot just consist of the meaningless positioning of the body towards an abstraction like "north" or "south." The understanding has to be engaged, and the "effectiveness" of the ritual is not in some magic transformation whereby a few movements of the limbs creates prosperity, but in a careful awareness of the meaning in things that brings about better focus and perceptiveness in everyday life.

"Six directions"— the usual four, plus vertically above and beneath—evoke a cosmic whole. In a different religion they might be six gods, six elemental powers, six dimensions of the life-force—but here the Buddha demystifies them into the six fundamental relationships. In what follows, the Buddha sounds surprisingly like a Confucian philosopher.

"And how, young man, does the noble disciple protect the six directions? These six directions should be known: mother and father as the east, teachers as the south, spouse and family as the west, friends and colleagues as the north, workers and servants as the lower direction, and ascetics and Brahmins as the upper direction.

"In five ways should a mother and father as the eastern direction be respected by a child: 'I will support them who supported me; I will do my duty to them; I will maintain the family lineage and tradition; I will be worthy of my inheritance; and I will make donations on behalf of dead ancestors.'

"And, the mother and father so respected reciprocate with compassion in five ways: by restraining you from wrongdoing, guiding you towards good actions, training you in a profession, supporting the choice of a suitable spouse, and in due time, handing over the inheritance.

"In this way, the eastern direction is protected and made peaceful and secure.

"In five ways should teachers as the southern direction be respected by a student: by rising for them, regularly attending lessons, eagerly desiring to learn, duly serving them, and receiving instruction.

"And, teachers so respected reciprocate with compassion in five ways: by training in self-discipline, ensuring the teachings are well-grasped, instructing in every branch of knowledge, introducing their friends and colleagues, and providing safeguards in every direction.

"In this way, the southern direction is protected and made peaceful and secure.

"In five ways should a wife as the western direction be respected by a husband: by honoring, not disrespecting, being faithful, sharing authority, and by giving [adornments].

"And, the wife so respected reciprocates with compassion in five ways: by being well-organized, being kindly disposed to the in-laws and household workers, being faithful, looking after the household goods, and being skillful and diligent in all duties.

In this way, the western direction is protected and made peaceful and secure.

"In five ways should friends and colleagues as the northern direction be respected: by generosity, kind words, acting for their welfare, impartiality, and honesty.

"And, friends and colleagues so respected reciprocate with compassion in five ways: by protecting you when you are vulnerable, and likewise your wealth, being a refuge when you are afraid, not abandoning you in misfortunes, and honoring all your descendants.

"In this way, the northern direction is protected and made peaceful and secure.

"In five ways should workers and servants as the lower direction be respected by an employer: by allocating work according to aptitude, providing wages and food, looking after the sick, sharing special treats, and giving reasonable time off work.

"And, workers and servants so respected reciprocate with compassion in five ways: being willing to start early and finish late when necessary, taking only what is given, doing work well, and promoting a good reputation.

"In this way, the lower direction is protected and made peaceful and secure.

"In five ways should ascetics and Brahmins as the upper direction be respected: by kindly actions, speech, and thoughts, having an open door, and providing material needs.

"And, ascetics and Brahmans so respected reciprocate with compassion in six ways: by restraining you from wrongdoing, guiding you to good actions, thinking compassionately, telling you what you ought to know, clarifying what you already know, and showing you the path to heaven.

"In this way, the upper direction is protected and made peaceful and secure."

Parents, children, teachers, students, husband, wife, friends, colleagues, employees, subordinates, spiritual mentors: we all have them. Each relationship has its unique problems and provocations, and at any given moment there is work to be done in each "direction." And the six directions make a whole: if even one of them is missing or messy, our contentment will be marred.

No other ancient text offers instruction on relationships as concise, complete, moderate, and feasible as this. We make allowances, as the Buddha would have, for changes in time and place: for example, "husband" and "wife" might be altered to different forms of conjugal relationship; "giving adornments" can be interpreted to include any act of generosity that makes the other person feel like a woman, a man, or just human. Throughout these, the emphasis on mutuality is remarkable. In the Hindu tradition, for example, there is a lot about what wife owes to husband, but barely anything on what husband owes to wife; or what responsibilities people in charge have towards employees (we might translate this to our responsibility to the nameless people who make our clothes or grow our food); or what spiritual teachers owe to their students. Even in the Confucian tradition, there is something excessive and one-sided about the duties of child to parent. In how many ancient traditions will we find a husband giving honor, respect, and authority to his wife?—or laborers and servants being treated with care and considerateness? Each "direction" is a balanced set—not as formal obligations or "laws," but as foundational considerations or "dhammas." If the sense of "dhamma" is missing, the relationship will go by rote and not be fulfilling; this is not about obeying rules, but about being realistic, since all functional relationships are built on reciprocal care.

Pervasive in these instructions is the call for kindness, that neglected virtue. "Kindly actions" and "kindly words" are easy enough to practice, and are the key to harmonious and pleasant daily relationships. The "six directions" concern social harmony as well as individual peace of mind; the latter is, for most of us, dependent on the former. But it goes beyond kindliness: in each case, our people are asked to respond "with compassion" towards us. It is as if we are all being asked to look beneath the surface of our social interactions and see the struggling human being, the one who is having a hard time—and this means all of us. Even workers and servants are asked to treat their masters with compassion. Without this exhortation to compassion, the Buddha's instructions to Sigalaka offer nothing more than an efficacious, respectful way to "manage" our relationships—but the need for compassion broadens the teaching to embrace the unmanageable, and the barely manageable, heart. Compassion requires understanding and empathy, a risky giving over of ourselves to the other person. [2]

The compassion of friends includes "being a refuge when you are afraid"—another extraordinary recommendation, both for ancient and for modern times, since people are generally reluctant to confess fears to one another. These fears may be specific—of enemies, of the law, of creditors—but they can also be deeply existential: fear of living, fear of hardship, fear of mortality, fear of the loss of meaning. In all of these respects friends

---

[2] "What a thing is relationship, and how easily we fall into that habit of a particular relationship, things are taken for granted, the situation accepted and no variation tolerated; no movement towards uncertainty, even for a second, entertained. Everything is so well regulated, so made secure, so tied down, that there is no chance for any freshness, for a clear reviving breath of the spring. This and more is called relationship. If we closely observe, relationship is much more subtle, more swift than lightning, more vast than the earth, for relationship is life. Life is conflict. We want to make relationship crude, hard, and manageable. So it loses its fragrance, its beauty. All this arises because one does not love, and that of course is the greatest thing of all, for in it there has to be the complete abandonment of oneself." J.Krishnamurti, from *J.Krishnamurti: A Biography* (Pupul Jayakar, 2000) chapter 23.

have been known to give comfort. It's striking that the Buddha places this responsibility firmly in the bosom of friends—not of parents, teachers, or spouse—perhaps because our friendships are uncomplicated by other tasks, such as running a household together. The "six directions" have to encompass all the ways in which we genuinely need, and need to open up to, one another.

All six directions have to be understood and practiced, both ways: this, says the Buddha, is what it means to worship the six directions. Each direction is difficult enough to "do" and provides abundant work for a lifetime, but what is even more astonishing is that a human being has somehow to juggle all six, in such a way that each direction is fulfilled and no single direction swallows the whole—which can easily happen, for example, when attention to a troubled family member becomes all-consuming. We need to fulfill all six directions to be happy; the neglect of just one will result in a niggling of the mind and perturbation of the heart. The Buddha refrains from adding more to Sigalaka's plate because it is already quite full. He could have said that the worship of the six directions is a way of developing character and disciplining the mind, to make it ready for a "higher" practice—but he doesn't. The cultivation of the six directions, with attention and with compassion, might be sufficient for a human life, and more than most people are willing to do. As with Confucius, we can learn from what the Buddha doesn't say.

3. Which Religion?
The Discourse to the Kalamas

When the refined Kalamas of Kesaputta hear that the Buddha has come to town, they immediately go to check him out. They have heard good things about him, but have grown wary of religious teachers and philosophers preaching their own views and denigrating those of others. Not all of them approach the new guru with reverence:

> On arrival, some of them bowed down to him and sat to one side. Some of them exchanged courteous greetings with him and, after an exchange of friendly greetings and courtesies, sat to one side. Some of them sat to one side having saluted him with their hands palm-to-palm over their hearts. Some of them sat to one side having announced their name and clan. Some of them sat to one side in silence.[1]

The reception ranges from respect, through courtesy and chilly politeness, to a silence either critical or openly hostile. They go straight to the point:

> Lord, there are some Brahmins and contemplatives who come to Kesaputta. They expound and glorify their own doctrines, but as for the doctrines of others, they deprecate them, revile them, show contempt for them, and disparage

---

[1] Thanissaro Bhikkhu (trans.), "Kalama Sutta: To the Kalamas," (*Anguttara Nikaya*, 3.65), *Access to Insight*, 1994. <https://web.archive. org/web/20131908090400/http://www.accesstoinsight.org/tipitaka/an/ an03/an03.065.than.html>.

them. And then other Brahmins and contemplatives come to Kesaputta. They expound and glorify their own doctrines, but as for the doctrines of others, they deprecate them, revile them, show contempt for them, and disparage them. They leave us absolutely uncertain and in doubt: Which of these venerable Brahmins and contemplatives are speaking the truth, and which ones are lying?

The Kalamas have rightly become nauseated by the vehement pontification and smug self-certainty of spiritual know-it-alls, and by fundamentalism in its various forms. They have stepped back from the furnace of belief and are looking for some way to cut through the blinding heat. Confronted with this challenge as soon as he sets foot in town, the Buddha—who sometimes comes across as one of those annoying men who have it all figured out—cannot now blithely put forth his own doctrine and criticize other views as mistaken; nor will he tell them—as he has told certain opinionated Brahmins elsewhere—that his path is not based on speculative views but on the understanding of suffering and the escape from it. He doesn't answer their question directly, but instead gives them a succinct list of criteria that deserves to be ruminated carefully. He begins, *"Of course you are uncertain, Kalamas. Of course you are in doubt. When there are reasons for doubt, uncertainty is born."* In all the big questions of life and death, how could there possibly be absolute certainty? One can always think of coherent alternatives to one's own beliefs, and even for the loudest fanatic the teeth of doubt can always be heard in the background, stubbornly gnawing.

> So in this case, Kalamas, don't go by reports, by legends, by traditions, by scripture, by logical conjecture, by inference, by analogies, by agreement through pondering views, by probability, or by the thought, 'This contemplative is our teacher.'

Reports, legends, traditions, scripture: in other words, don't just believe what you've been told, what is affirmed through common opinion, what has been handed down through the generations, what is claimed to be revealed truth, or what you find in a book. This group broadly includes testimony, authority, and everything written or posted on the Internet. In ordinary life, we rely upon such sources all the time—newspapers, word of mouth, science documentaries, textbooks, what our friends tell us, Google, Wikipedia—but in matters of real importance to us, we need more rigorous standards. For example, if we are diagnosed with cancer, will we not also want to see the evidence for ourselves and not just believe the experts?

At this point the Cartesian modern will say, "So the Buddha is telling us to use our own minds and think for ourselves!" But he includes "our own minds" in the next set: *logical conjecture, inference, analogies, "pondering views," and probability*. What are these five things? By "logical conjecture" he means surmise, speculation—as when we employ arresting imagery to picture the origin of the universe or the features of heaven and hell. "Inference" encompasses syllogistic reasoning—as it is used, for example, in Anselm's beautifully solid proof for the existence of God. Who, after studying Anselm's ontological argument, is ever convinced by it, and who does not vaguely feel that he is being tricked either by Anselm or by the rules of the mind? "Analogies" can also be compelling enough to make us think we know—for instance, when scientists talk about the idea of "gravity" using analogies like "attraction" and "repulsion," are they aware that such language is actually figurative? "Agreement through pondering views" would include the body of what we call "knowledge" that has been arrived at through deliberate collective activity over time—such as academic consensus in a given field, or "science" (as when opinion pieces use the phrase "according to science"). "Probability" is also to be doubted, for there are many occasions when the truth behind what happens is improbable, and when what should be so according to common sense is in fact not so, either because many things are not commonsensical or because our own common sense is not the authority it seems to us to be. In sum, we are being asked not to believe our own minds *simply*. With the first set of sources, the Buddha is urging us to question everything we see and hear; with the second, to question everything we think. It is an insincere learner who will question everyone and everything but not himself.

So what is left? Do we have no certain ground to stand upon? What about the guru? No, says the Buddha, we cannot rely on "this contemplative is my teacher": there is no external source of truth who will solve everything for us, just as we have no "equipment" or resource, material or immaterial, that will infallibly give us access to the truth. Because the Kalamas already suspect this, they are suspicious of anybody who claims to know the truth about important matters. The Buddha, brilliant teacher as he is, begins this dialogue by making explicit what they already know but do not necessarily want. If the discourse ended here, we would be left with a counsel of thoroughgoing skepticism, and probably be resigned to not knowing anything.

Instead, what the Buddha does is to adjust the focus.

> When you know for yourselves that, 'These qualities are unskillful; these qualities are blameworthy; these qualities are criticized by the wise; these qualities, when adopted & carried out, lead to harm and to suffering' — then you should abandon them.

This seems at first a strange statement to follow the list of possible sources of cognition. The conversation moves to a consideration of greed, aversion, and delusion, not as abstract ideas, but experiences: when we experience these, what do we find? The

Buddha is always an empiricist: look at your experience and study it—what do you see there? All the keys we need to hold are within our own experience, so it is with our experience that we need to start. *When you know for yourselves* is the crucial clause (to which the opinion of "the wise" is important but subordinate), and if we know nothing *for ourselves* we can have no touchstone for what we know through the conventional sources of knowledge previously enumerated. Our own experience has to be digested and understood first. This is not an "anything goes" view; rather, we will know some important things if we patiently and thoroughly examine our lives.

> "What do you think, Kalamas? When greed arises in a person, does it arise for welfare or for harm?"
> "For harm, lord."
> "And this greedy person, overcome by greed, his mind possessed by greed, kills living beings, takes what is not given, goes after another person's wife, tells lies, and induces others to do likewise, all of which is for long-term harm and suffering."
> "Yes, lord."
> "Now, what do you think, Kalamas? When aversion arises in a person, does it arise for welfare or for harm?"
> "For harm, lord."
> "And this aversive person, overcome by aversion, his mind possessed by aversion, kills living beings, takes what is not given, goes after another person's wife, tells lies, and induces others to do likewise, all of which is for long-term harm and suffering."
> "Yes, lord."
> "Now, what do you think, Kalamas? When delusion arises in a person, does it arise for welfare or for harm?"
> "For harm, lord."
> "And this deluded person, overcome by delusion, his mind possessed by delusion, kills living beings, takes what

is not given, goes after another person's wife, tells lies, and induces others to do likewise, all of which is for long-term harm and suffering."

"Yes, lord."

"So what do you think, Kalamas: Are these qualities skillful or unskillful?"

"Unskillful, lord."

"Blameworthy or blameless?"

"Blameworthy, lord."

"Criticized by the wise or praised by the wise?"

"Criticized by the wise, lord."

"When adopted and carried out, do they lead to harm and to suffering, or not?"

This exchange seems glib and unconvincing if it is read swiftly, but if we take each question as followed by a long pause, perhaps even a pause lasting days, as we go through particular instances of greed and its effects in our lives, only then will the Buddha's exhortation to *know for yourselves* make sense. The point is to reflect honestly on what really happens and on the nature of consequences. This one page about greed, aversion, and delusion may point to everything we need to know about the causes of suffering, but the reflection is something that we need to do. To read the Sutta, we have to learn to read ourselves. We might end up not agreeing with the Buddha in all details, but at least our disagreement will be grounded in our own experience and subject to continued investigation.

The Buddha will go on in the rest of this discourse to talk about positive states of mind and how good, how pleasant, they are in themselves: even if there is no reward for being good in this life or in the afterlife, it will have been good for its own sake. This is no "speculative view"; the entire drift of this discourse is that we can know this is so by rigorously examining our own experience. Here there is no description of advanced mental states,

no teachings about non-self or dependent origination, no analysis of craving and attachment. The Buddha has not answered the
Kalamas' question; instead, he has "reset" it, bringing it down to
earth or, as Confucius puts it, "near at hand." He has taught
them what to do if they want to answer, for themselves, their
own question.

4. Shopping for a Spiritual Teacher

In the "Vimamsaka Sutta" (or "The Inquirer"), the Buddha springs an audacious challenge on his disciples:

> "Bhikkhus, a bhikkhu who is an inquirer, not knowing how to gauge another's mind, should make an investigation of the Tathāgata in order to find out whether or not he is fully enlightened."[1]

How do you know if a teacher is the "real thing" or not? If you're serious, you'll try to find out, and not just swallow what you're told. The problem is, since you're not enlightened yourself and cannot see into the mind of anyone else, how will you ever know if your guru is everything he is cracked up to be? If you're a real inquirer, and not just somebody who wants comfortable or pleasant states of mind, you will investigate—and the Buddha tells you how to go about it. The list of criteria that follows is further proof of the Buddha's common sense and mental clarity, and it also implicitly contains a profound challenge to the seeker who wants to *know* the truth and not just to be told.

> Are there found in the Tathāgata or not any defiled states cognizable through the eye or through the ear?

First, when you watch this prospective teacher carefully, does anything strike you as wrong or "off"?—not only the obvious defilements like greed or lust, but subtle attachments, lying, deviousness, narcissism? "Cognizable through the eye or the ear" seems to cover everything done or said, but also gestures and fa-

---

[1] Bhikkhu Bodhi (trans.), "The Inquirer" (*Majjhima Nikaya,* 47), SuttaCentral. https://suttacentral.net/en/mn47.

cial expressions. Second, *Are there found in the Tathāgata or not any mixed states cognizable through the eye or through the ear?* This can be interpreted in at least two ways: Is the teacher's conduct consistently good, or is there unsteadiness and inconsistency—for example, is he often loving but sometimes choleric and spiteful? Or is his action sometimes ambivalent in quality—for instance, showering one disciple with so much praise and affection that the disciple is blinded by this excess of welcome attention? I once witnessed how a revered swami, all sweet and chuckly to his audience, viciously scolded and slapped the small boy who brought him his tea because it wasn't warm enough. This may indicate a "mixed state" at best, a "defiled state" at worst.

Supposing you don't see mixed or defiled states: *Are there found in the Tathāgata or not cleansed states cognizable through the eye or through the ear?* There is a bright, loving energy about this teacher, no obsessiveness or insecurity, nothing unhinged, nothing off—but also, *Has this venerable one attained this wholesome state over a long time or did he attain it recently?* One has to observe the teacher carefully over a long time to know that his goodness of character is firmly and deeply established. The assumption is that no one is simply born spiritually realized; we all have to put in work and effort over time, and it takes time for virtue to become rooted.

When you have found someone impressive and are certain that the admirable character is stable and settled in virtue, examine how fame and prestige have affected him. *Has this venerable one acquired renown and attained fame, so that the dangers connected with renown and fame are found in him?* We have seen in our own time many instances of the corruption of gurus through adulation and the absence of critical scrutiny: sex scandals, money scandals, and drug abuse. If the character of the teacher has blind spots and immaturities, fame and adoration will manifest and magnify them. Does the teacher, for instance, consider himself immune to sin and error, and does he listen well to other people, or does he constantly presume that he knows what is in their minds? When contradicted or disagreed with, how does he react? The Buddha is asking us to watch meticulously. I wonder if there is even one other ancient sage with the courage and foresight to point out the liabilities of spiritual celebrity.

Is this venerable one restrained without fear, not restrained by fear, and does he avoid indulging in sensual pleasures because he is without lust through the destruction of lust? That is to say, how is his behavior in private, when he is not constrained by fear of the law or social pressure? The Buddha is in fact asking us to pry: it is not enough to know that the teacher is trustworthy on the surface, because we need to know that he is thoroughly trustworthy—that he is good because he is good, and not because he is afraid of getting caught. We should not take this on faith, and obviously, to know such things we need to observe for a long time. We also need to see if the teacher is partial to people, if he is fair, if he treats all disciples equally: *Whether that venerable one dwells in the Sangha or alone, while some there are well behaved and some are ill behaved and some there teach a group, while some here are seen concerned about material things and some are unsullied by material things, still that venerable one does not despise anyone because of that.* Disciples are going to be flawed and in need of guidance, and if you are going to be one of them you have to know that the teacher will give you the same attention as everyone else and not have favorites. A true teacher does not despise imperfect people.

When you strike lucky and find a teacher you can trust, you develop "faith" in the teacher only as you progress in your learning through his instruction: *The Teacher teaches him the Dhamma with its higher and higher levels, with its more and more sublime levels, with its dark and bright counterparts. As the Teacher teaches the Dhamma to a bhikkhu in this way, through direct knowledge of a certain teaching here in that Dhamma, the bhikkhu comes to a conclu-*

sion about the teachings. He places confidence in the Teacher. It will have taken years to get to this point. Only now, *Bhikkhus, when anyone's faith has been planted, rooted, and established in the Tathāgata through these reasons, terms, and phrases, his faith is said to be supported by reasons, rooted in vision, firm.* "Reasons, rooted in vision" means "reasons that emerge from the depths of our direct experience": finding your teacher is not about blind faith, surrender to charismatic authority, or trust in someone else's revealed truth. It requires careful and thorough scrutiny, in which you don't just "believe" but verify for yourself that this person is worthy to guide you in the search for the most important things.

I can imagine that a spiritual seeker's first reaction on hearing this would be shock: *It's going to take me so much time and so much work to find a spiritual teacher!* Just thinking about the Buddha's criteria, it seems unlikely that there could be anyone who could satisfy all of them—and even if such a person were to exist, would I ever meet him, would I be fortunate enough to live in the same century or on the same continent? The Buddha's own disciples are being provoked: how indeed do they know that their own teacher is the real thing? In an age of upheaval, when old interpretations are threatened and everyone is confused, it is natural for a person to want certainty, and to crave a "still point in a turning world." This is no less true of the Buddha's time than of ours. For us the certainty might come in the form of one of the many churches or scientific dogmas; for his disciples the truth had to be found in one of the sixty-two or more views of life that were being vigorously promulgated. His culture was one where a "view" usually centered upon a teacher, and students were then drawn to this teacher if they wanted the key to the door of their lives. The *Vimamsaka Sutta* is utterly characteristic of the Buddha in that it gives his students no easy answer, and throws them back upon their own seeing and hearing. Throughout the Pali Nikayas the emphasis is on knowing for yourselves: there is no shortcut to experiencing for ourselves, thinking for ourselves, and seeing from where we actually are. This involves painstaking, frustrating, risky attentiveness. A teacher may tell us something, but until we see it for ourselves we do not really know it—and when we look into our own lives, trying to see, we may guess but we cannot pre-know what we will see. The Buddha is deeply aware of the terrible temptations of authority. Because we are afraid of our own solitude, and are insecure about what we see for ourselves, we crave the reassurance and support of a teacher. This makes it all too easy for us to replace our own insight with the words of the teacher, to triangulate our own experience against the fixed points of those words, and never to stray too far from them. The disciple's anxiety about how her own experience meshes with the teachings becomes a screen that eventually separates her from her own insight, which is no longer anything more than the shadow cast by the teacher. The Buddha's project requires us to meet our own experience head on and to stare it in the face; for this reason, in sutta after sutta, he has to undermine his disciples' dogged efforts to squeeze a "view" out of him that they can cling to for safety. He wants us to become spiritually adult, capable of self-reflection and self-correction. It is not that the Buddha's guidance should count for nothing with us, but that that guidance can speak to us only if we are truly engaged, from moment to moment, with our own awareness. Fearful impatience drives us toward quick answers and clear teachings, but we need to look at that impatience too and ask what it really is.

5. Samvega: The Great Unsettling

Each of us can think of a handful of moments in our lives when everything dramatically changed and there was no going back to what we were in the previous moment. We experience these irrevocable transitions as simultaneously feelings and cognitions: disturbance, shock, sadness, euphoria, a profound unsettling both of our emotions and our understandings. It is an "unsettling" precisely because afterwards we can no longer take for granted that we are at home in our lives; we have been uprooted, and now feel lost. While this experience of loss is always uncomfortable and often painful, it is also essential to our emotional, intellectual, and spiritual growth—and continued growth means staying attuned to the agitation and shock of the breakthrough moments.

Anton Chekhov's very short short story, "The Beauties" (1888), gives exquisite expression to what happens when a sensitive soul meets beauty for the first time. The speaker is a teenager who, accompanying his grandfather on a trip through the dusty countryside, sees an unattainably beautiful Armenian girl at a farmhouse and feels the encounter as something like a blow that then becomes a permanent open wound:

> At first I felt hurt and abashed that Masha took no notice of me, but was all the time looking down; it seemed to me as though a peculiar atmosphere, proud and happy, separated her from me and jealously screened her from my eyes.
> "That's because I am covered with dust," I thought, "am sunburnt, and am still a boy."
> But little by little I forgot myself, and gave myself up en-

tirely to the consciousness of beauty. I thought no more now of the dreary steppe, of the dust, no longer heard the buzzing of the flies, no longer tasted the tea, and felt nothing except that a beautiful girl was standing only the other side of the table.

I felt this beauty rather strangely. It was not desire, nor ecstasy, nor enjoyment that Masha excited in me, but a painful though pleasant sadness. It was a sadness vague and undefined as a dream. For some reason I felt sorry for myself, for my grandfather and for the Armenian, even for the girl herself, and I had a feeling as though we all four had lost something important and essential to life which we should never find again. My grandfather, too, grew melancholy; he talked no more about manure or about oats, but sat silent, looking pensively at Masha. [1]

Even the grandfather is not immune to the contagion. *Neither desire, nor ecstasy, nor enjoyment*: in other words, the feeling has nothing to do with what we normally think of as Eros or the Romantic, but is more like the otherworldly rapture felt by Confucius when, having heard the music of Shao for the first time, he forgot the taste of meat for three months. *I thought no more now of the dreary steppe, of the dust, no longer heard the buzzing of the flies, no longer tasted the tea, and felt nothing except that a beautiful girl was standing only the other side of the table.* Yet what he feels is not "ecstasy" or some stereotypical spiritual bliss. It is the transcendental sadness of a cherished veil being torn away to reveal an emptiness where the familiar face had been. After this, one can no longer be "happy," because something essential is always missing and will not be restored through time or the wisdom of age: *he talked no more about manure or about oats, but sat*

---

[1] Anton Chekhov, "The Beauties" (1888), translated by Constance Garnett. http://www.eldritchpress.org/ac/beauties.htm.

silent, looking pensively at Masha.

Chekhov offers no resolution to this. His deep insight in these few pages is to include in the experience both teenager and grandfather, impressionable youth and hardened age. The sadness envelopes both the beholders of beauty and the beauty itself, because everyone sooner or later finds himself and herself engulfed in a yearning that cannot be satisfied.

In "The Beauties," Chekhov gives modern voice to an ancient discovery. Plato describes this yearning several times—for instance, in the *Symposium*, where Alcibiades laments Socrates' destruction of his peace of mind:

> For when I hear him I am worse than any wild fanatic; I find my heart leaping and my tears gushing forth at the sound of his speech, and I see great numbers of other people having the same experience. When I listened to Pericles and other skilled orators I thought them eloquent, but I never felt anything like this; my spirit was not left in a tumult and had not to complain of my being in the condition of a common slave: whereas the influence of our Marsyas here has often thrown me into such a state that I thought my life not worth living on these terms. [2]

Compare this to the effect on the protagonist of Chekhov's masterpiece "The Kiss" of a fleeting encounter with an unknown woman in the dark:

> And the whole world, the whole of life, seemed to Ryabovitch an unintelligible, aimless jest.... And turning his eyes from the water and looking at the sky, he remembered again how fate in the person of an unknown woman had by chance caressed him, he remembered his summer dreams

---

[2] Plato, *Symposium*, translated by W.R.M.Lamb, Loeb Classical Library (Cambridge: Harvard University Press, 1925) 215e-216a.

and fancies, and his life struck him as extraordinarily mea-
gre, poverty-stricken, and colourless....[3]

Although this experience most commonly occurs through
the powerful smiting of Eros, it can happen in an encounter with
art, the holy, or both together.[4] Eric Gill describes the effect of
hearing Gregorian chant: "At the first impact I was so moved by
the chant ... as to be almost frightened ... This was something
alive ... I knew infallibly that God existed and was a living God."
This response articulates powerfully one important aspect of the
experience: the sense of becoming painfully open to something
more real, more alive, than life itself—in the face of which everything in our lives shows up as insufficient. We are dealing here
with no mere *passion*—a passive reaction to some stimulus—but
an emotion that is at the same time an insight, just as the crack-
ing of an egg is at the same time sound and fracture.

There is a word for the experience I have been trying to describe: in Pali, it is *samvega*. Ananda Coomaraswamy, the great
Indian writer on art, explores the idea of Samvega in an essay
called "Aesthetic Shock": *Samvega is a state of shock, agitation,
fear, awe, wonder or delight induced by some physically or mentally
poignant experience. It is a state of feeling, but always more than a
merely physical reaction. The "shock" is essentially one of the realization of the implications of what are strictly speaking only the aesthetic
surfaces of phenomena that may be liked or disliked as such.*[5] While it

---

[3] Chekhov, "The Kiss" (1887), translated by Constance Garnett
(1919) https://en.m.wikisource.org/wiki/The_Kiss_(Chekhov/ Garnett).

[4] Eric Gill, *Autobiography* (Biblia and Tannen, New York, 1968)
187.

[5] Ananda Coomaraswamy, "Aesthetic Shock" (1943). https:// ar-
chive.org/stream/AKCoomaraswamy/Coomaraswamy,%20A.K.%20-
%20The%20Essential%20Ananda%20K.%20Coomaraswamy%20(2004
)_djvu.txt.

is part of a deep aesthetic response, the range of samvega encompasses all experiences that have power to jolt us into estrangement with our lives. Coomaraswamy traces the word through a selection of Sanskrit and Pali texts:

> The Pali word samvega is often used to denote the shock or wonder that may be felt when the perception of a work of art becomes a serious experience. In other contexts the root vij, with or without the intensive prefix sam, or other prefixes such as pra, "forth, "implies a swift recoil from or trembling at something feared. For example, the rivers freed from the Dragon, "rush forth" (*pra vivijre*, Rg Veda X.III.9), Tvastr "quakes" (*vevijyate*) at Indra's wrath (ibid. I. 80.14), men "tremble" (*samvijante*) at the roar of a lion (Atharva Veda VIII.7.15), birds "are in a tremor" at the sight of a falcon (ibid. VI.21.6); a woman "trembles" (*samvijjati*) and shows agitation (*samvegam âpajjati*) at the sight of her father-in-law, and so does a monk who forgets the Buddha (Majjhima Nikâya, I.186); a good horse aware of the whip is "inflamed and agitated" (*âtâpino samvegino*, Dhammapada 144); and as a horse is "cut" by the lash, so may the good man be "troubled" (*samvijjati*) and show agitation (*samvega*) at the sight of sickness or death, "because of which agitation he pays close heed, and both physically verifies the ultimate truth (*parama saccam*, the 'moral') and presciently penetrates it" (Anguttara Nikâya II.116). "I will proclaim, " the Buddha says, "the cause of my dismay (*samvegam*), wherefore I trembled (*samvijitam mayâ*): it was when I saw people floundering like fish when ponds dry up, when I beheld man's strife with man, that I felt fear" (or "horror"), and so it went "until I saw the evil barb that festers in men's hearts" (Sutta Nipâta, 935938).

When a sensitive person encounters a work of art and feels shaken, such that he is unable to return to his daily routines with contentment, let alone pleasure, and such that most other works of art now seem trivial — that is samvega. What Coomaraswamy describes is primarily the unique aesthetic agitation given by the greatest works of art, but this agitation — as Chekhov's "The Beauties" shows — is felt also in encounters with people and with the beautiful. Sudden realizations of insufficiency can also pierce us in our everyday lives, as when something said or done creates a disillusionment that engulfs us and leaves us incapable of going on with "business as usual."

A scholar of the Pali Suttas, Thanissaro Buikkhu, puts it thus:

> Samvega was what the young Prince Siddhartha felt on his first exposure to aging, illness, and death. It's a hard word to translate because it covers such a complex range — at least three clusters of feelings at once: the oppressive sense of shock, dismay, and alienation that come with realizing the futility and meaninglessness of life as it's normally lived; a chastening sense of our own complacency and foolishness in having let ourselves live so blindly; and an anxious sense of urgency in trying to find a way out of the meaningless cycle. This is a cluster of feelings we've all experienced at one time or another in the process of growing up, but I don't know of a single English term that adequately covers all three. It would be useful to have such a term, and maybe that's reason enough for simply adopting the word samvega into our language. [6]

Thanissaro shrewdly notes that samvega is usually felt as threatening to individual or societal life, and strategies are in place for suppressing it or rendering it innocuous: you are unhappy because you are being unreasonably idealistic, and you need to find contentment by lowering your expectations; stop worrying so

---

[6] Thanissaro Bhikkhu, "Affirming the Truths of the Heart," Access to Insight, 1997. http://www.accesstoinsight.org/lib/authors/thanissaro/affirming.html.

much and let yourself have fun and enjoy life; go to therapy and have yourself adjusted back into functionality; understand that everything is made by God and is all good; live in the Now, find a way to enjoy doing the dishes, and don't allow yourself to be distracted by an intellectualized Big Picture. All of these are familiar and complex strategies for anaesthesia: we can numb the pain by obscuring and fuzzing up the insight—make the pain smaller by making the heart smaller.

Buddhism gives a discipline and a path in which we can drink our samvega straight. Thanissaro argues that it is important not to forget the feeling that brought us onto the path; indeed, we need to keep it alive and stay in touch with it. But it needs to be balanced with a positive emotion—in this case, *pasada*, another complex set of emotions usually translated as "clarity and serene confidence." Without something like *pasada*, one can become mired in a turbulent dismay of samvega—whereas *pasada* without samvega would be a hollow cheerfulness that only looks like courage.

In "The Beauties," Chekhov doesn't give us any solutions or resolutions: the encounters he describes open up a big hole in life, and once it is open it cannot be closed again. Samvega is the discovery of this hole; its shock and agitation are what impel us into the strenuous quest for truth and for the beauty of truth, and after its tremors it is difficult to repose any longer in comfort or pleasure. This is a good thing: we are given a standard that prevents us from ever being content with the merely pretty or pleasing. In my own life as a reader, writer, lover of art and music, and educator, I remember clearly the samvega moments that pushed me over the threshold, and have seen that my students and colleagues in the Liberal Arts nearly all have known samvega too; that is one reason we get along so well. The danger for us lies in our occupational habituation to deeply moving texts of all kinds, so that we become dulled to samvega—taking small daily doses of the poison, as it were, until it becomes harmless to us, even pleasant. If samvega ever becomes "safe"—something that we can calmly contemplate without a hint of disturbance—if we can read "The Beauties" and only recognize the sadness conceptually without being perturbed by it, then we will find that we have been drugged back into thinking that the realm of manure and oats is the only one there is. If there is one emotion that needs to be attended to and nourished throughout a philosophic or literary life, it is samvega—because it is what brought us here and what keeps us honest.

Until we experience for ourselves the great unsettling of samvega, we are not ready to embark on the strenuous spiritual journey: we are too satisfied with our lives as they are, too much at home in the worlds we are given. The fruit is not yet ripe. This is why the Buddha never tries to convert anyone; he knows that when we are ready, we will find ourselves naturally torn and dislocated from our familiarity with the world. And when we have been dislocated, discovering ourselves as strangers in a strange land, we will finally be able to *hear* an objective diagnosis of our illness and will have genuine interest in being healed.

Part 2

Foundations of the Practice

In the following essays I attempt to penetrate the fundamental aspects of the Buddha's curriculum of disciplined awareness, through which we will learn to see more clearly who we are and what causes unhappiness. The foundation of all Buddhist practice is the cultivation of sustained awareness as an art of living, and in this cultivation we all have to begin in the same way.

6. Minding Your Mouth: The Buddha's Simple but Powerful Advice about Effective Speech

Likewise, the tongue is a small part of the body, but it makes great boasts. Consider what a great forest is set on fire by a small spark. —James, 3:5

Let thy speech be better than silence, or be silent. —Dionysius Of Halicarnassus

If you want to stop suffering, says the Buddha throughout the Discourses, there is an eightfold path of practice to that end, consisting of right view, right motivation, right speech, right action, right livelihood, right effort, right mindfulness, and right *samādhi*.[1] With its connotations of orthodox correctness, the word "right" is actually a misleading translation of the Pali word *samma*, which means "perfected, completed, consummated." The point is that working on ourselves entails a gradual completing of what we are supposed to do, until we find ourselves "fulfilled" and "accomplished" with regard to the eight limbs of the path. It is "eightfold" in the sense not of eight steps to be taken consecutively, but of eight branches to one trunk, or eight tributaries flowing into one river: each of these is essential to getting you there, but all eight have to be involved. Among the eight, some are more spiritually "glamorous" than others, and of the homely ones none seems plainer than "right speech" or *samma-vaca*. Yet *samma-vaca* turns out to be a powerful practice that we can do

---

[1] Bhikkhu Bodhi (trans.), "The Discourse on Mindfulness Meditation," *Majjhima Nikaya* 10, SuttaCentral https://suttacentral.net/en/mn10.

anywhere, anytime, and with anyone, transforming us both inside and out.

And what is samma-vaca? asks the Buddha. *Refraining from lying, divisive speech, harsh speech, and meaningless speech. This is called 'samma-vaca'.* The statement seems so innocuous and unobjectionable, but let's see how the Buddha unpacks it.

In one of the shorter suttas from the *Anguttara Nikaya*, the Buddha engages Cunda the Silversmith in a discussion of Hindu rituals of purification, and then describes what purification means for a follower of the new path.[2] Quite simply, the Buddha undertakes "purification" of three things: bodily action, verbal action, and mental action. If these are "impure," all the rituals with water and fire will do us no good; and if these are "pure," the rituals with water and fire will be redundant. In other words, working on what we do, say, and think is a sufficient practice for "purification," but without working on what we do, say, and think, no ritual practice is sufficient. *Samma-vaca* gives us an excellent example of the kind of thing the Buddha means by "purification."

Many have remarked that if you cannot control your mouth, you have no hope of controlling your mind. Most people spend the first decade of their lives learning Elementary Right Speech: how to interact politely, respectfully, inoffensively, when to speak, when not to speak, and so on. Then we spend another decade on Intermediate Right Speech, which involves techniques of argumentation and presentation, the expression of more complex feelings and ideas, the heuristic and investigative uses of language. Some of what we study on these two levels is bottom-

---

[2] Thanissaro Bhikkhu (trans.), "The Cunda Kammaraputta Sutta: To Cunda the Silversmith," *Anguttara Nikaya*, 10.176, Access to Insight, 1997. http://www.accesstoinsight.org/tipitaka/an/an10/an10.176.than.html#speech.

less; even something as simple as when to speak and when not to speak cannot be determined by formula, and the knowledge of "when" is refined over a lifetime. But are we ever taught that we can use language in such a way as to improve ourselves or harm ourselves? Here we begin to enter on Advanced Right Speech, in which we become more consciously skilled with our words. Each act we commit feeds and waters a sprout that can grow into a habit; insofar as thoughts and statements are also actions, they too have the power to grow into habits and thus change us. When we become aware of the effects of our words, both on ourselves and on others, we realize that every word we utter makes a mark, and nothing we say can be deleted. The Buddha points out that our own speech can make us "impure"—confused, muddy, self-evading, increasingly unable to separate truth from untruth. His own words on the matter are hard to improve upon and worth listening to carefully:

> "And how is one made impure in four ways by verbal action? There is the case where a certain person engages in false speech. When he has been called to a town meeting, a group meeting, a gathering of his relatives, his guild, or of the royalty [i.e., a royal court proceeding], if he is asked as a witness, 'Come and tell, good man, what you know': If he doesn't know, he says, 'I know.' If he does know, he says, 'I don't know.' If he hasn't seen, he says, 'I have seen.' If he has seen, he says, 'I haven't seen.' Thus he consciously tells lies for his own sake, for the sake of another, or for the sake of a certain reward. He engages in divisive speech. What he has heard here he tells there to break those people apart from these people here. What he has heard there he tells here to break these people apart from those people there. Thus breaking apart those who are united and stirring up strife between those who have broken apart, he loves factionalism, delights in factionalism, enjoys factionalism, speaks things that create factionalism. He engages in abu-

sive speech. He speaks words that are harsh, cutting, bitter to others, abusive of others, provoking anger and destroying concentration. He engages in idle chatter. He speaks out of season, speaks what isn't factual, what isn't in accordance with the goal, the Dhamma, and the Vinaya, words that are not worth treasuring. This is how one is made impure in four ways by verbal action."

The four ways are: (1) telling falsehoods, by which we deliberately relax our commitment to truth and eventually even become so tied to subtly evolved fictions that we can no longer notice when we might be fooling ourselves; (2) saying things that are certain to cause strife, contention, and bad feeling, thus destroying social harmony by creating a miasma of mistrust—and at the same time turning ourselves into the kind of spiteful little creature who delights in dragging other people down; (3) uttering words designed to hurt and upset, sowing internal strife in those around us, and undermining their capacity for contentment; and (4) filling precious silence with babble that can matter to no one, just to hear our own voices or to cover over a silence in which anxiety might arise. This fourth destructive way is the hardest for a modern to understand, so accustomed are we to our sound-realms constantly being filled with "entertainment" or commentary; silence disturbs us, it is "awkward." Just from a single day's experience with social media posts, I can cull dozens of examples of each of the "four ways": posts that are careless of truth and factually reckless, posts that are sure to turn some group of people against another and drive them both farther into contention, posts that we know will hurt and anger someone, and posts that are just for posting's sake, for "fun." The effect of all of these together is unproductive emotional entanglement and mental confusion.

When we become more disciplined and scrupulous with our words, the opposite happens, and we find ourselves becoming better people:

> And how is one made pure in four ways by verbal action? There is the case where a certain person, abandoning false speech, abstains from false speech. When he has been called to a town meeting, a group meeting, a gathering of his relatives, his guild, or of the royalty, if he is asked as a witness, 'Come and tell, good man, what you know': If he doesn't know, he says, 'I don't know.' If he does know, he says, 'I know.' If he hasn't seen, he says, 'I haven't seen.' If he has seen, he says, 'I have seen.' Thus he doesn't consciously tell a lie for his own sake, for the sake of another, or for the sake of any reward. Abandoning false speech, he abstains from false speech. He speaks the truth, holds to the truth, is firm, reliable, no deceiver of the world. Abandoning divisive speech he abstains from divisive speech. What he has heard here he does not tell there to break those people apart from these people here. What he has heard there he does not tell here to break these people apart from those people there. Thus reconciling those who have broken apart or cementing those who are united, he loves concord, delights in concord, enjoys concord, speaks things that create concord. Abandoning abusive speech, he abstains from abusive speech. He speaks words that are soothing to the ear, that are affectionate, that go to the heart, that are polite, appealing and pleasing to people at large. Abandoning idle chatter, he abstains from idle chatter. He speaks in season, speaks what is factual, what is in accordance with the goal, the Dhamma, and the Vinaya. He speaks words worth treasuring, seasonable, reasonable, circumscribed, connected with the goal. This is how one is made pure in four ways by verbal action."

Here we are introduced to the rare person who can always be counted on to be truthful and honest; who nonetheless never speaks in such a way as to cause discord, and is both good at and enjoys making friendships; whom people routinely seek out because of her sincerity, kindness, good nature, and encouragement; who is always to the point, and always worth listening to. This is an image of a wonderful, lovable human being—the kind of person we would want for a friend, and also one that we can all aspire to become.

The beauty of such a path is that it can be practiced, for at the beginning of each day we can actually articulate to ourselves an intention to work on the four aspects of *samma-vaca* with regard to the particular people and situations of our daily lives; and at the end of the day we can reflect, evaluate in detail whether we succeeded or not, and then decide what we need to do to improve. It is the conscious application of our reflective intelligence that makes this a practice, and not just the spontaneous play of natural gifts. Did I tell the truth? Was I right to tell my friend X what my other friend Y had said about him? Did I hurt W's feelings and make it harder for him to speak with me? Did I just waste an hour chatting about politics on Facebook? Underlying all of these questions is the bigger question about motivation: Why did I speak, what in me needed to say this? In thinking about these things and trying to cultivate lucidity regarding our own actions, we gradually become smarter about ourselves, more sensitive to other people, and more nuanced in our actions.

A habit of self-reflection tends to make us more moderate and judicious, but being mindful of our mouths develops the special kind of intelligence that is attuned to the intricate mysteries of language. We are never done with the work of *samma-vaca*; it becomes more challenging and more interesting the better we become at it, and it is work that never stops expanding our minds and hearts. I still think about ways I could have said things better fifty years ago, and the good or bad effect of things that were said to me long ago—for every utterance is a small seed that cannot be prevented from growing into something of consequence. The discipline of *samma-vaca* has its focus on particular instances, but each of these instances is full of meaning.

Speaking well depends on listening well, and learning how to listen may be one of the hardest things a human being has to do. We are generally poor listeners from impatience, arrogance, desire, and fear: impatience, because we are eager to say our own thing or because we have some other task to check off; arrogance, because it is natural for people to assume they are qualified to judge others, so that we already "know" what our interlocutor will say and whether it is worth listening to; desire, because we want to hear ourselves corroborated; and fear, because there are things we know we don't want to hear. When we are silent, is it because we are listening or because we are waiting to speak? When we speak, are we responding to the person in front of us, or merely reacting or deflecting? If we are habitually unresponsive to people and situations, we cannot be sincere practitioners of *samma-vaca*. It will be obvious that our silences are also included in this, because all silence expresses something, and some silences are more eloquent than words. To the extent that many silences are in fact preparations for speech, words exist in a continuum from intuition, to thought, to utterance—which means that the thoughtful practitioner of *samma-vaca* must attend to what precedes speaking as much as to speaking itself.

Thus the art of speaking well includes the complementary art of listening well. Both of these arts cannot be taught as an arsenal of techniques and strategies to master. For example, we can know all there is to know about different methods of beginning an argument, but how do we know when to start and how to choose the words that will move this particular person? Or we can have a large enough vocabulary and wide experience of life to understand the words that are spoken to us, but how do we intuit the real intentions behind the words—such as whether the speaker is friendly or unfriendly towards us—let alone understand why the intentions are what they are? If we have no insight into these deeper matters, we are unlikely to address this interlocutor effectively in speech.

But how do we learn such things? It would seem that there is no shortcut; we learn from paying attention to every interaction and reflecting afterwards on what went right or wrong. We learn from mistakes, and also from letting others point out our mistakes: when we said things poorly, when we misunderstood, when we completely misjudged an interlocutor, when we failed to sustain a harmonious relationship. Mistakes and failures make up the rich seedbed of self-reflection and improvement. Because of this, *samma-vaca* is a practice that will tend to make a person more grounded, generous, humble, attentive, observant, present—and at the same time, more reflective, imaginative, far-sighted, open to other people and to other possibilities. It is a richly rewarding practice for a thoughtful person, and a salutary discipline for a less thoughtful person, because it encompasses so many other virtues. Indeed, *samma-vaca* is itself a mindfulness practice that tends to get instant feedback because it occurs in the moment, with other people.

The wonder is that every human being can do this practice in some way; each of us is capable of trying to listen well and to speak well, and of the self-reflection that these require. Even when we find ourselves perplexed in certain situations and unable to see clearly, we can always consult our friends, who can be helpful in getting us to see what we did wrong and how we could do better. In the Pali Discourses, the Buddha's gift is twofold: a vision, and a practice. He always gives us something we can *do*—indeed, that we can start doing *now*, wherever we are, by ourselves. There is no need to wait for anything or anyone.

7. Enlightenment in Just Seven Days!
Mindfulness (1)

The words "mindful" and "mindfulness" go back centuries in English.[1] Before Buddhism was translated into English, "mindfulness" ranged in meaning from "remembrance" to "attentiveness" to "taking thought," and to be "mindful" of something was to "turn the mind" towards it. Only in 1881 was the word "mindfulness" used (by T.W. Rhys Davids) to translate the word *sati*—probably after much vacillation and casting around for alternatives. The word *sati* is itself the Pali version of the Vedic Sanskrit word *smrti*, which means "memory, remembrance, calling to mind" and was the shorthand term for the body of Hindu scriptures that were not divinely revealed but formed through human recollection. But what does "mindfulness" have to do with "remembering?"—after all, we nowadays associate mindfulness with being "present," whereas remembering is about the past.

Our primary source for the practice of "mindfulness" is the *Satipatthana Sutta* ("Mindfulness-Foundation," *Middle Length Discourses*, 10), in which the Buddha describes a revolutionary new solution to the problem of suffering. Although "mindfulness" has become almost a daily catchphrase for us, it is important to understand just how original, how truly radical, this practice was when it first appeared. No other ancient thinker, East or West, came up with anything remotely resembling it. In the following essays I'll be looking closely at the practice itself

---

[1] *What is a man, that mindful thou art of him?* (Wycliffe Bible, Psalms 8:6, c.1382) *There was no mindfulness amongst them of running away.* (Holinshed, *Histories*, 1577).

and what it means, but the focus of this essay will be the striking claims made in the frame of the Sutta.

After setting the time and place, it begins:

> [T]he Blessed One addressed the bhikkhus as follows: "This is the only way, O bhikkhus, for the purification of beings, for the overcoming of sorrow and lamentation, for the destruction of suffering and grief, for reaching the right path, for the attainment of Nibbana, namely, the Four Arousings of Mindfulness."[2]

The only way is a surprising phrase, because in other Suttas the Buddha appears to have suggested to different people different approaches to the practice. The phrase translated is *ekayano maggo*, which literally means "only way" or "one path." Reluctant to go with this too restrictive reading, other translators have come up with variations such as "one-way path" (no going back), or path that goes in one direction only, straight to the truth without beating around the bush:

> This is the direct path for the purification of beings, for the overcoming of sorrow and lamentation, for the disappearance of pain and distress, for the attainment of the right method, and for the realization of Unbinding — in other words, the four frames of reference.[3]

Or it is a path on which all beings are united in the same project—that is, to end suffering, with respect to which we are all in the same boat:

---

[2] Soma Thera, "The Discourse on the Arousing of Mindfulness," in *The Way of Mindfulness: The Satipatthana Sutta and its Commentary*, Access to Insight, 1998 http://www.accesstoinsight.org/lib/authors/soma/wayof.html#discourse.

[3] Thanissaro Bhikkhu, *Satipatthana Sutta: Frames of Reference*, Access to Insight, 2008. http://www.accesstoinsight.org/tipitaka/mn/mn.010.than.html.

Monastics, this is the path where all things come together as one, to purify sentient beings, to make an end of pain and sadness, to get past sorrow and lamentation, to reach the way, to witness Nibbāna; that is, the four kinds of mindfulness meditation.[4]

It is impossible not to notice that in all three translations the wording of the final goal feels very different: the attainment of Nibbana, the realization of Unbinding, to witness Nibbana. The first suggests the arrival at a positive state, the second a kind of negation or removal, and the third a contemplative dwelling on an object. Unless we have ourselves practiced and find ourselves closer to what is being described in these phrases, there is really no way we can judge between the different translations or know if they are indeed different. "Getting past" sorrow and lamentation also sounds very different from the "destruction" of those feelings. The benefit to us of these variations is that they show us that even for experienced meditators and great Pali scholars there is room for considerable difference of interpretation—and this knowledge in turn throws us back onto our own experience and judgment. One thing they all agree upon is the idea of purification: this is the one path or direct path for the purification of beings. What might *purification* mean here? We shall try to find out.

The other part of the frame, the end of the sutta, coming after the four kinds of mindfulness have been described in detail, also has two very startling assertions:

Let alone seven years, anyone who develops the four kinds of mindfulness meditation in this way for six years ... five years ... four years ... three years ... two years ... one year

---

[4] Bhikkhu Bodhi, *The Discourse on Mindfulness Meditation*, Sutta-Central. https://suttacentral.net/en/mn10.

... Let alone one year, anyone who develops the four kinds of mindfulness meditation in this way for seven months may expect one of two results: final enlightenment in this very life, or if there is anything left over, non-return. Let alone seven months, anyone who develops the four kinds of mindfulness meditation in this way for six months ... five months ... four months ... three months ... two months ... one month ... half a month ... Let alone half a month, anyone who develops the four kinds of mindfulness meditation in this way for seven days may expect one of two results: final enlightenment in this very life, or if there is anything left over, non-return. (Bhikkhu Bodhi)[5]

Final enlightenment in this very life, or if there is anything left over, non-return: although right now, from where we are in our practice, we might have no capacity whatsoever to understand the meaning of these words, we have to notice the phrase *in this very life*. What we are promised here is not attainment after death, or in the next life or world—but in *our* life, *this very* life. It's an audacious claim. Moreover, if we do what we are asked to do in this sutta, we can attain this at the end of seven days. A week. To a skeptic, this sounds like the kind of self-help hype we see occasionally online or in magazines: "Enlightenment in 'Just' 7 Days!"

The more you read the Pali Suttas, the more you realize that these are not texts that typically indulge in wild hyperbole. They often sound like instruction manuals—dry, terse, unemotional, matter-of-fact—and seem deliberately to reject the emotional uplift of other, so-called spiritual texts. The Buddha is always scrupulous in his choice of words. When he says it is the *only* way, he might mean that; and when he says that seven days might be enough, we must bear in mind that he is not prone to

---

[5] Ibid.

exaggeration. If we take him seriously, we will see that the dozen or so pages that follow hold the beating heart not only of the Buddha's teaching but also of his experience—and if we listen to them deeply, these pages might indeed be all we need.

In what comes next, we are provoked to attend and get closer to the four essential dimensions of our own experience—and the first of these is the experience of being in a body.

8. *The Underrated Wonder of Breathing:*
Mindfulness (2)

Those encountering the *Satipatthana Sutta* for the first time are often surprised to find that such an influential text—central to Theravada, Mahayana, and Zen—makes no arguments and offers no vision of the ultimate nature of reality, but instead consists of twenty-one exercises for focused contemplation. These exercises have been subjected to hundreds of thousands of pages of often conflicting commentary, and some of them have become the central practice for entire Buddhist communities. In this essay and the ones to come, I intend to read the *Satipatthana Sutta* in a spirit of humble, naïve inquiry, hoping to show that even for a newcomer to these practices the Buddha's words do indeed make sense in terms of ordinary human experience—which they in turn illuminate. I make no claims to having a comprehensive overview of the path, and am content here to dwell on the exercises that seem particularly rich and powerful to me.

The Daoist sage Zhuangzi gives us this dismally concise summation of a normal human life:

> We sleep and our spirits converge; we awake and our bodies open outward. We give, we receive, we act, we construct: all day long we apply our minds to struggles against one thing or another—struggles unadorned or struggles concealed, but in either case tightly packed one after another without gap. The small fears leave us nervous and depleted; the large fears leave us stunned and blank. Shooting forth like an arrow from a bowstring: such is our presumption when we arbitrate right and wrong. Holding fast as if to sworn oaths: such is our defense of our victories. Worn away as if by autumn and winter: such is our daily dwin-

dling, drowning us in our own activities, unable to turn back. Held fast as if bound by cords, we continue along the same ruts. The mind is left on the verge of death, and nothing can restore its vitality. [1]

Our lives are constructed on a foundation of internal and external insecurities. Because this foundation is always shaking, made up as it is of changing realities and mental projections, the structure we put on it is also shifting, unstable, subject to a constant process of frenzied construction and repair. How can we save ourselves from drowning in this frenzy?

For a reader accustomed to philosophical traditions—both East and West—that begin from the premise that the body is a dark, unknowable, painful thing that hinders light and knowledge and must be transcended if we are to attain the higher realms of Truth and Goodness, the Buddha's opening recommendation has to be startling: a practitioner has to begin by "contemplating the body in the body."

> And how, O bhikkhus, does a bhikkhu live contemplating the body in the body?
> Here, O bhikkhus, a bhikkhu, gone to the forest, to the foot of a tree, or to an empty place, sits down, bends in his legs crosswise on his lap, keeps his body erect, and arouses mindfulness in the object of meditation, namely, the breath which is in front of him.[2]

The very first step is to remove ourselves from the realm of our frantic activity, finding some place where we will not be interrupted, and sit. The foot of a tree is a wonderful place for this because from a tree we can learn, by osmosis, to be still. It is not

---

[1] *Zhuangzi: Essential Writings,* translated by Brook Ziporyn (Hackett: Cambridge, 2009) 9-10.

[2] Soma Thera, 1998.

that a tree is inactive; there is infinite life in its bark and foliage, infinite movement in the air and light playing about the leaves and in the fluids coursing through the veins, and unimaginable power in every cell and in the coordination of the cells to keep such a huge thing upright for so long amidst all the buffetings of weather. Yet the tree lives, bursting to fullness with all this energy, and has no need to bustle around achieving tasks. Sitting by this tree, we can draw strength and focus from it as we arouse mindfulness or *sati*. We bring our attention to bear on our first object of meditation: breath.

> Mindful, he breathes in, and mindful, he breathes out. He, thinking, 'I breathe in long,' he understands when he is breathing in long; or thinking, 'I breathe out long,' he understands when he is breathing out long; or thinking, 'I breathe in short,' he understands when he is breathing in short; or thinking, 'I breathe out short,' he understands when he is breathing out short.[3]

This seems at first ridiculously simple and tedious, and a person reading it for the first time might nod politely and pass on, because this is too easy and obvious; or might try it for a few minutes and then move to something more interesting. If we do react in this way, we will have missed the point completely. What the Buddha is offering here is the antidote to our toxic frenzy. We are submerged, asphyxiated, in the high dramas and cyclical intensities of the fabrications that we take to be our lives. Because we have lost ourselves in a fog where we can no longer differentiate fantasy from reality, the only way to obtain clarity is to find something we are certain about. One such thing is the fact that we will die, and the Buddha will invite us to chew on this soon; but another is the undeniable fact that as I am writing and as you are reading, we are both breathing. Not only is

---

[3] Soma Thera.

breathing happening, but we are capable of experiencing it, of bringing our attention to bear on it.

This is so obvious that we should be shocked that we need a teacher to point it out to us, but it is testimony to the genius of the Buddha that the first exercise on the path involves breathing: something we are all doing anyway, whether we want to or not, and therefore a universal phenomenon that we have access to and can contemplate—anyone, anywhere, anytime. Again, this is blindingly obvious—but a wise person is not afraid of the obvious, especially if it tells us what we need to listen to but so far have failed to hear. The practice can start *here, now*; in the case of breathing, we need nothing extra and have no excuse to procrastinate.

For a student coming to this from another religion, the Buddha's matter-of-fact way of talking about breathing is also striking: he is discussing *only* breathing, and not turning the breath into something high-flown and spiritual, such as *prana* or the mystical breath-energy of the universe. The Buddha makes no cosmic claims in these exercises, and if we undertake this exercise thinking that in breathing we are uniting with the transcendent breath of the world-spirit, we will have again missed the point. He is asking us to locate ourselves in the earthy and mundane, not to glorify ourselves. This is why he specifies contemplating the body in the body: not the divine principle in the body, or the body in the divine principle, or the body mixed up with feelings and thoughts, or the body as an idea ("mechanical"/"organic")—simply the body, in itself, nothing more and also nothing less. Moreover, what the bhikkhu does is to observe the breath as it is; he doesn't seek to slow it down or to influence it in any way, with the aim of creating a different emotional state. In the paragraph just quoted, the qualifiers are "long" and "short," but there could be other qualifiers --for instance, steady or unsteady, forceful or weak, full or thin, different at the end than at the beginning, and so on. The more we practice this, the more we will notice—and our breathing becomes high definition breathing, rather than the haphazard low resolution affair it used to be. The key is that we are sitting and engaging; it is not about *doing* anything, but about seeing accurately what is there in front of us, beyond the mediating ideas we may have of it. Some have described mindfulness as "bare attention," where "bare" means stripped of extraneous accessories and adornments, naked, pure.

When we consciously experience breathing in this naked way, one of the first things to dissolve is the conception of breathing as respiration, as mere inhalation and exhalation of air by nose, mouth, and lungs. The air is experienced just beyond the nose, and we become aware of the coolness around the nostrils, the motion of the nostrils, our hairs, the distinctive feel of the air as it moves to the back of the nose, and so on—until, the intercostal muscles and ribcage expanding, we can feel the drawing down of the diaphragm as the entire torso breathes. With the exhale, it is easier to feel the whole body participating, as it relaxes in the toes, fingers, and face. It is not possible to describe fully what we discover when we engage our breathing with single-minded attention, and as we become more skilled and more sustained in our attending, we can see that every single breath is unique:

> "Experiencing the whole body, I shall breathe in,' thinking thus, he trains himself. 'Experiencing the whole body, I shall breathe out,' thinking thus, he trains himself. 'Calming the activity of the body, I shall breathe in,' thinking thus, he trains himself. 'Calming the activity of the body, I shall breathe out,' thinking thus, he trains himself.
> "Just as a clever turner or a turner's apprentice, turning long, understands: 'I turn long;' or turning short, understands: 'I turn short'; just so, indeed, O bhikkhus, a bhikkhu, when he breathes in long, understands: 'I breathe in

long'; or, when he breathes out long, understands: 'I breathe out long'; or, when he breathes in short, he understands: 'I breathe in short'; or when he breathes out short, he understands: 'I breathe out short.' He trains himself with the thought: 'Experiencing the whole body, I shall breathe in.' He trains himself with the thought: 'Experiencing the whole body, I shall breathe out.' He trains himself with the thought: 'Calming the activity of the body I shall breathe in.' He trains himself with the thought: 'Calming the activity of the body I shall breathe out.'[4]

Thus breathing becomes an art, something to practice and become good at. The image of the skilled turner is evocative: imagine a turner on an ancient lathe, holding it steady with both feet while his hands turn the wood, the entire body alert and concentrated at an insubstantial edge—there, where the wood meets the blade. The true craftsman respects and follows the nature of the wood, bringing out its internal potential without forcing anything; and the action of turning is fluid, continuous, unhesitating. A stranger to wood and to woodworking would be quite blind to fine distinctions in grain and shape that the turner can perceive with his whole body; skilled turning is not an act of mere manual production, but a creative and cognitive coming together of body and spirit. This is what breathing can become when we engage with it. We discover too that all sense of agency has been lost. The true artist is the first to tell you that he didn't *do* anything; whatever it was happened *through* him, and he himself doesn't understand what happened but could see it happening. Breathing is obviously an autonomic function: as long as we are alive it happens, we were not there when it started and will not be there when it ends. In the meantime we can ride the breath like the swimmer in Zhuangzi who is at home in the

---

[4] Soma Thera.

fiercest rivers because he is not afraid of following the undertows wherever they take him. As with any skill, the better you get at it, the more enjoyable and satisfying it becomes—and the remarkable gift given in this one page on breathing is that an action so ordinary, so barely noticeable, yet going on in us all the time, can become a source of pleasure and joy.

The first exercise of the *Satipatthana* concludes with a passage that gets repeated throughout the sutta with regard to other exercises as well:

> Thus he lives contemplating the body in the body internally, or he lives contemplating the body in the body externally, or he lives contemplating the body in the body internally and externally. He lives contemplating origination-things in the body, or he lives contemplating dissolution-things in the body, or he lives contemplating origination-and-dissolution-things in the body. Or indeed his mindfulness is established with the thought: 'The body exists,' to the extent necessary just for knowledge and remembrance, and he lives independent and clings to naught in the world. Thus, also, O bhikkhus, a bhikkhu lives contemplating the body in the body."[5]

This is an invitation to reflect and examine, to hold what we have experienced and rotate it in our mind's eye slowly, carefully, so that we understand it three-dimensionally and from various angles: the interior experience, its manifestation externally and objectively, the relation of those two, how a breath begins and continues and ends, or how there isn't really a beginning and end because "breathing" is not a thing but a confluence of a myriad things in reciprocal activity. I am a being who breathes at this

⁵ Nyanasatta Thera (trans.), *Satipatthana Sutta: The Foundations of Mindfulness*, Access to Insight, 1994. http://www.accesstoinsight.org/lib/nyanasatta/wheel019.html.

moment, in this place, having among my conditions a body that can take in air and a universe that has the air I can take in; and both this body and this universe abide in an infinity of conditions, all in action so that this, just this, can happen. Thus *sati* is truly remembrance, a recollection of what we actually are, and it is only through this deliberate exercise of focused attention that we will begin to remember our own lives.

However, the paragraph ends with a sober caution: it is easy to get carried away from this experience and to lose ourselves in theories and speculations that arise from the thoughts we will inevitably generate from the exercise. Instead, we reflect *to the extent necessary just for knowledge and remembrance*, and no matter how excited we become at our own discoveries, there is no need to impress, no need to spread the word, no neediness at all: *he lives independent and clings to naught in the world.*

9. Finding Our Bodies: Mindfulness (3)

If we are not breathing, we are dead—a fact so obvious as to be hardly worth saying. But because it is true, the observation of breathing can be the primary discipline in the cultivation of attentiveness: it is available to us at no cost, and can be experienced at any time and place with our whole bodies. But our bodies are also susceptible to observation anywhere, anytime. At every moment we find ourselves in some physical position; even our motions of transition between different positions are themselves positions, although continuous and less easily defined. The second exercise in the *Satipatthana Sutta* is therefore the turning of attention to bodily positions and movements, called the *iriyapatha* or "ways of movement." You will see this word translated often as "postures" or "deportments," but the former has connotations of stasis and Yoga *asanas*, and the latter is an archaic term that can also include "bearing." The classical reference points for the *iriyapatha* are standing, sitting, lying down, and walking:

> And further, O bhikkhus, when he is going, a bhikkhu understands: 'I am going'; when he is standing, he understands: 'I am standing'; when he is sitting, he understands: 'I am sitting'; when he is lying down, he understands: 'I am lying down'; or just as his body is disposed so he understands it. [1]

The last clause of this encompasses any positioning of the body: sprawling, leaning, running, jumping, swimming—the entire astonishing spectrum of motions and positions that our

---

[1] Soma Thera, *ibid.*

bodies may undergo in the course of the day. In this long sentence the verb "understands" occurs five times—but what exactly can the Buddha mean by it?

On first reading, it appears that we are being asked to be aware of what our bodies are doing and to register the awareness with a simple thought: "Now I am seated, now standing up, now walking..." This itself is instructive, because we are capable of passing through the day mostly unconscious of the lay of our bodies, since we are usually focused on something else; our bodies exist just below the conscious threshold, as vehicles for our mental preoccupations. To divide our bodily dispositions into the four categories of standing, sitting, lying down, and walking is clearly too crude to express much of what we do—for instance, I know that I sit in at least eight different ways, and have several rhythms for walking, most of which have no name. If the practice is to attach a label to each of my body positions and then move on to the next one, it will be nothing more than a practice of replacing experiences with words and then skating over a thin surface of words—which might be attractive to a person eager to transcend physical experience by attenuating its intensity. Not only does this feel like an unsatisfying strategy of avoidance, but it goes against the mandate for direct experience that we were given in the exercise of mindful breathing.

What might it be to "understand" standing, for example? In the Chinese art of Qigong there is a set of meditative exercises consisting wholly of standing in various positions. The simplest possible version of this is just to stand naturally, feet shoulder width apart, hands hanging by your side, without moving, breathing in a relaxed way.

If you have never done this, you will find that simply standing still for fifteen minutes is very difficult; after about three minutes, for no special reason, you will be fighting the urge to shift. Focusing on breathing then becomes a helpful distraction that temporarily calms the agitation; counting breaths gives us something productive to "do" and might even provide us with a "goal." Such attempts at diversion remove us from the tedium of the raw experience, but sooner or later we become bored with breathing or counting and have to return to our bodies. At that point we might experience strain: tension in back and shoulders from habitual poor posture, achy knees and feet, fatigue, and resistance to standing still. Nothing is more strenuous than not moving. If we keep standing through our discomfort, and try to pay attention to the physical sensations in joints and muscles, we also notice how they change over time and never stay the same. They are also all interconnected through the whole body, and tension in the face might be related to stiffness in the feet and calves. Standing for an hour makes us extremely aware of every inch of body; indeed, it is a very difficult feat to accomplish if the anatomy is not perfectly aligned and both body and mind as relaxed as possible. At first, a cultivation of this kind is quite difficult, but only because we are not used to deliberate engagement with the body. Dancers, actors, musicians, martial artists, and gymnasts are habituated to it, and develop formidable strength and stamina through detailed, methodical movement. The rest of us, preoccupied with activities that take us away from our bodies, have to struggle more, but with practice it becomes easier. If we begin to "understand" standing, we will naturally start to perceive all our other movements more lucidly and vividly. No two steps will be alike, each pushup or squat will be new, and each moment incomparable.

One practical effect of bringing such focused attention to our bodies is greater delight and satisfaction in living, as we learn to notice minute transitional motions, and gains in balance, stability, and proprioception. For physical health it is essential, because if we are wholly unaware and outside of our own bodies we will injure ourselves no matter what we are doing, especially sitting. Yet much of our environment is constructed so that we can ignore our bodies: office chairs shaped in such a way that our backs automatically take care of ourselves, shoes with soles so padded that we don't have to feel the hard ground, weightlifting machines on which we only have to sit and push without engaging most of the body. A world constructed like this makes it easy for us to lose ourselves in our own entertaining cloud-pictures.

The section ends with the same refrain that ended the meditation on breathing:

> Thus he lives contemplating the body in the body internally, or he lives contemplating the body in the body externally, or he lives contemplating the body in the body internally and externally. He lives contemplating origination-things in the body, or he lives contemplating dissolution-things in the body, or he lives contemplating origination-and-dissolution-things, in the body. Or indeed his mindfulness is established with the thought: 'The body exists,' to the extent necessary just for knowledge and remembrance, and he lives independent and clings to naught in the world." Thus, also, O bhikkhus, a bhikkhu lives contemplating the body in the body.[2]

Which of us has not experienced the shock, in seeing a video of ourselves standing or walking, of finding that what we do is utterly different from what we had imagined ourselves doing? We think that our posture has improved, and that we have been working hard to feel a vertical and well-held backbone, but according to the incontrovertible evidence of film, there we are with the same old unappealing and insalubrious slouch. On receiving this shock, we may have extra incentive to bridge the chasm between our internal and external apprehensions of ourselves. But again, the text warns us against over-engaging and

---

[2] Soma Thera.

becoming compulsive about contemplation: we do it *to the extent necessary just for knowledge and remembrance.*

The *Satipatthana* then passes immediately into a short meditation that gives a different articulation of embodied awareness:

> And further, O bhikkhus, a bhikkhu, in going forwards (and) in going backwards, is a person practicing clear comprehension; in looking straight on (and) in looking away from the front, is a person practicing clear comprehension; in bending and in stretching, is a person practicing clear comprehension; in wearing the shoulder-cloak, the (other two) robes (and) the bowl, is a person practicing clear comprehension; in regard to what is eaten, drunk, chewed and savored, is a person practicing clear comprehension; in defecating and in urinating, is a person practicing clear comprehension; in walking, in standing (in a place), in sitting (in some position), in sleeping, in waking, in speaking and in keeping silence, is a person practicing clear comprehension.[3]

What is "clear comprehension"?—or, in another translation, "full awareness"? We seem to have expanded from "contemplating the body in the body" to contemplating it in relation to everything around it, both spatially and causally. Thus, for example, in defecating, we have trained to become acutely aware of the bodily positioning—which includes the precise adjustments of seating, in coordination with the delicate interior pressures that give rise to bowel movement and that vary sometimes hugely from day to day, expressing fluctuations in our entire physical health. But this is only partial mindfulness: now we also have to remember the full context of our action—the need to maintain detailed cleanliness of the space, the careful placement of paper, soap and towel for the next person, the conserving of water in

---

[3] Soma Thera.

view of its source and scarcity, the knowledge of where the waste is going, scrupulousness in the selection of toilet paper and of other requisites, for the sake of doing least harm to the world and to other people. Merely to pay attention to the body and give no thought to its position in the web of relations and consequences would not be truly mindful, but rather a kind of self-absorption that mimics mindfulness. With regard to mindfulness in the toilet, we have all seen that it can take a decade or more for a young human being to master most of the details, but even as rational adults most people live as if flushing their poop down the white ceramic hole somehow magically makes it all disappear or become someone else's problem. It takes sustained and persistent effort to achieve "clear comprehension" of our embodied activity, but such effort is what it takes to get closer to our own existence and live it, not just float vaguely above it.

However, in my thinking about breathing and bodily activity, have I succumbed to he seduction of giving meditation some kind of goal or reward?—health, happiness, the discovery of truth, a richer life. In finding that an increased sensitivity to what is happening leads to a more interesting and vivid relationship to my own physical existence, have I sublimated the discomfort of meditation into a species of thrilled fascination? I am very aware that I have understated the acute discomfort of meditation, which is felt within the first few minutes of attempted practice: we hit a wall that we push against with all our might, and that wall is boredom. The contemplating of breathing and of bodily movement is overwhelmingly boring; when undertaken wholeheartedly, it does not move us to any higher realm but remains with itself. Ultimately, breathing is breathing, defecating defecating, and that is all—no more and no less. This does not change over years of practice, and no matter how many moments of significant discovery and delight I have experienced, I always return eventually to "Enough. I can't do it any more today," or my mind quietly wanders off by itself because it cannot bear the tedium. We have to bring it gently back to its yawning abyss of ennui and let it dwell there, because—beyond all the radiant pleasures and understandings—the real work of mindful meditation is to take us out of our dreams and face ourselves for once.

10. Deliberate Disenchantment: Mindfulness (4)

The Buddha is the first great empiricist: he never asks us just to believe anything he says, or to accept statements as true based on reason or inference alone. His *Satipatthana Sutta* is primarily a sequence of exercises for experiencing what makes us up. With breathing and our bodily movements, we feel and watch—but we are not given any conclusions about them. This is partly because the Buddha wants us to win back our own eyes and see for ourselves, and partly because the aim of the exercises is not to generate and amass propositions but to get us closer to our own existence—to see clearly what is there. In these exercises he can be called a "radical empiricist," by William James' standard: *To be radical, an empiricism must neither admit into its constructions any element that is not directly experienced, nor exclude from them any element that is directly experienced.*[1] However, the next few exercises on "contemplating the body in the body" are not simply empirical in that imagination is called upon to aid experience.

Most of us take great care with our appearance; if we think we don't, it is probably because over the decades the care we take has become second nature and we forget how much mental energy has gone into the cultivation of our clothing styles and of good hygiene habits. The investment is more than practical: if someone criticizes or mocks our physical appearance, most of us will be mortified or upset—and if our looks are praised, we will immediately find ourselves liking the praiser. We are also emotionally invested in our physical health—hence the trepidation

---

[1] William James, *Essays in Radical Empiricism* (London, 1912) 42.

we feel when going to the doctor or dentist for a checkup, even though we know rationally that learning the truth is a good thing; and hence too our disproportionate demoralization on hearing even slightly bad news about our bodily condition. As we get older, the fear and dismay intensify, while at the same time we know that it is increasingly reasonable to expect a diagnosis of serious illness. In all these cases, we live as if we cherish an image of our bodily selves that requires corroboration from others and that cannot bear to be disturbed. This self image, which we secretly love and enjoy tending to, looks out at us from the bathroom mirror, and from a mirror in our minds. Even in the case of people who claim to hate their own bodies, their disproportionate emotional vehemence still testifies to attachment to a self-image, which torments because it is loved. The daily unconscious hold of the idealized body-image generally comes to the surface at the shock of discovering that others do not see us as we see ourselves. When such shocks occur, we tend to be upset for a short while before the wound seals up again. It is our unconsciously coddled and caressed body-image that makes us oblivious to the fact that others see us as older or younger than we feel ourselves to be, to our terrible posture and awkward walk, to our distinctive smells, to the little tones and gestures that annoy or offend those closest to us. Obviously, armored as we are with an image of our bodies that we cannot see, it is very difficult for us to attain any true mindfulness of body. How do we break through the armor?

The Buddha recommends an exercise in systematic disenchantment, in which we dismantle this body that we are so fond of, and consider its constituent parts. It cannot be a purely empirical exercise, because we do not have direct perception of most of our interior organs, but we can combine what we perceive and what we know about, to make the composite body an object of contemplation:

> And further, O bhikkhus, a bhikkhu reflects on just this body hemmed by the skin and full of manifold impurity from the soles up, and from the top of the hair down, thinking thus: 'There are in this body hair of the head, hair of the body, nails, teeth, skin, flesh, fibrous threads (veins, nerves, sinews, tendons), bones, marrow, kidneys, heart, liver, pleura, spleen, lungs, contents of stomach, intestines, mesentery, feces, bile, phlegm, pus, blood, sweat, solid fat, tars, fat dissolved, saliva, mucus, synovic fluid, urine.'[2]

It is easy to see how this reflection would be characterized as a cultivation of "revulsion," but revulsion plays only a small part in the whole process. Most people are not revulsed by hair or skin, and the idea of their own teeth, sweat, and bones creates no perturbation. But it is not the *idea* of them that we are being asked to contemplate. When we see our own blood, many of us have to repress panic; there is panic too if we slip and fall and find that there is a bone sticking out of our leg, or if we are in a public place and cannot control our bowels. Things like bile, pus, and phlegm are fine if they stay where they are supposed to, under cover, but their obtrusion into our attention is distressing. When there is some kind of disruption in our bodies, we always become miserable at what we now have to attend to—because we expect everything to keep its place, so that the designated surface remains a surface, and what is meant to be under it stays concealed. The shattering of place, of surface, reveals to us our own components removed from their normal background. This exercise pulls everything out and turns it into a list, where each item comes under a general heading but no relationship between items is specified. We become this list of unrelated items, most of which we do not like to examine directly; someone else's liver in a science museum is acceptable, but not our own liver in its

---

[2] Soma Thera.

dark red, rubbery splendor.

Doing this contemplation just once is an interesting, provoking exercise, but if we were to undertake this disintegration regularly, how would it affect the self-image? When we dress in the morning and check ourselves in the mirror, what would we see?—the same old Me, or a collection of parts to be tended? If someone were to joke about our appearance, would we be bothered any more, knowing as we do that there is no one thing to "appear" and to defend from mockery? A nose is a nose, a heart is a heart, and all of us have the same fluids. In this contemplation, we have demystified our bodies—contemplating "the body in the body," as opposed to body as amplification of ego.

I had an analogous experience in a firearms training class. Before the class, if I were to find a Colt 45 lying on a table, I would approach it hesitatingly with beating heart, and pick it up with fear; during the class, I learned how to check to see if it was loaded, how to render it harmless, how it works, and how to take it apart; after the class, I could pick up any gun calmly as just another piece of machinery that could be harmful in ignorant hands. It is ignorance that fuels the mystique. The Buddha has given us a way to pick up the body, unload it, and dismantle it: we have one good strategy for dispelling the mystique of our own bodies.

He goes further and asks us to learn to view our bodies dispassionately, with no more emotion than we would feel in opening a bag of rice: nothing here to love or hate.

> Just as if, O bhikkhus, there were a bag having two openings, full of grain differing in kind, namely, hill-paddy, paddy, green-gram, cow-pea, sesamum, rice; and a man with seeing eyes, having loosened it, should reflect thinking thus: 'This is hill paddy; this is paddy, this is green-gram; this is cow-pea; this is sesamum; this is rice.' In the same way, O bhikkhus, a bhikkhu reflects on just this body

hemmed in by the skin and full of manifold impurity from the soles up, and from the top of the hair down, thinking thus: 'There are in this body: hair of the head, hair of the body, nails, teeth, skin, flesh, fibrous threads (veins, nerves, sinews, tendons), bones, marrow, kidneys, heart, liver, pleura, spleen, lungs, contents of the stomach, intestines, mesentery, feces, bile, phlegm, pus, blood, sweat, solid fat, tears, fat dissolved, saliva, mucus, synovic fluid, urine.'[3]

The Buddha reinforces the lesson by following it up with another, slightly more abstract, disintegrative exercise. In this one we are asked to envision the body as broken down into its fundamental functions and characteristics, feeling no more about it than if we were to see all these "modes" laid out in front of us like meat at a butcher's stall:

> And further, O bhikkhus, a bhikkhu reflects on just this body according as it is placed or disposed, by way of the modes of materiality, thinking thus: 'There are in this body the mode of solidity, the mode of cohesion, the mode of caloricity, and the mode of oscillation.'
>
> O bhikkhus, in whatever manner, a clever cow-butcher or a cow-butcher's apprentice, having slaughtered a cow and divided it by way of portions, should be sitting at the junction of a four-cross-road; in the same manner, a bhikkhu reflects on just this body, according as it is placed or disposed, by way of the modes of materiality, thinking thus: 'There are in this body the mode of solidity, the mode of cohesion, the mode of caloricity, and the mode of oscillation.'"[4]

He ends these sections with the usual exhortations to take a

---

[3] Soma Thera.
[4] Soma Thera.

more rounded reflection of these aspects of the body, and also not to get carried away—contemplating *only to the extent necessary just for knowledge and remembrance,* no more and no less. This is an important caution, because the reader coming to this for the first time can easily mistake it for a reductive view of life—as indeed many Buddhists do, who assert to us with contempt that "the body is nothing but a sack full of fluids, etc." You will hear this from Hindu holy men too. Yet the Buddha in these passages is neither giving us a view of life nor trying to express the essence of a body: he is offering a simple exercise, which anyone can do, that enables us to "contemplate the body in the body," as distinct from its complex mystique.

In other suttas deliberate disenchantment is presented as a useful strategy to combat potential attachments. For example, when you feel yourself about to fall into an intense and dangerous infatuation with a person you are in two minds about, apply the meditation to your new object of attachment; at the same time, apply it to yourself, in case you were hoping that this person would find you extraordinarily attractive and special. The exercise is meant to get you to see "the other side" of things, the back side, and not the side that is a colorful display of ego to ego. We break down the human being into a list of all its parts, so that we are less likely to be magnetized by any one aspect. In applying the same meditation to someone you fear—for example, the intimidating boss or neighbor—the mystique evaporates on seeing the other body as exactly the same as yours in its physical constitution. On the level of body, there is nothing remarkable to love or to loathe.

An exercise like this gains power if, through frequent repetition, it becomes habitual—so that we do it naturally, in the moment, and not just retrospectively as an antivenin to attachments that have already arisen. Thus, when invited to a party, we are already lucid about our own physical limitations and are no longer susceptible to the erotic frisson of meeting new bodies; or, when in middle age we go for a medical checkup and are not in the least worried about nasty new discoveries but, on the contrary, scientifically interested in seeing the current state of our body for what it really is; or, when facing the imminent failure of some crucial body part, we are already content with the fact that the body is an agglomeration of parts that will not hold together forever. This is sanity with respect to the body. The alternative is a body mystified by ego and entangled in the ego's crazy dramas.

If we succeed in separating the body from the realms of emotion and thought, and no longer see the body as the medium for expressing "who we are," we will achieve a life of greater equanimity and clarity—but at what cost? For one thing, in the eradication of personal vanity and of attachment to corporeal beauty, we will have doused the fires of eros—but is that a madness we would want to live without?

Montaigne recounts the story of two ancient madmen who are cured of their ailments:

> This man [Lycas], though otherwise of very regular conduct, living quietly and peacefully in his family, failing in no part of his duty toward his own and toward strangers, preserving himself very well from harm, by some alteration of his senses had stamped in his imagination this hallucination: he thought he was perpetually at the amphitheaters watching entertainments, spectacles, and the finest comedies in the world. After being cured of this peccant humor by the doctors, he nearly sued them to make them restore him to the pleasures of these fancies.

> Alas, you have not saved me, friends, quoth he,
> But murdered me, my pleasure snatched away,
> And that delusion that made life so gay. (Horace)

His delusion was like that of Thrasylaus, son of Pythodo-
rus, who tricked himself into believing that all the ships
that put out of the port of Piraeus and came in there were
working only in his service; he rejoiced in the good fortune
of their voyages and welcomed them with joy. When his
brother Crito had had him restored to his better senses, he
regretted that state of mind in which he had lived full of joy
and free from all trouble. It is what this old Greek verse
says, that there is great advantage in not being so wise,

In heeding nothing lies the sweetest life. (Sophocles)

And Ecclesiastes: "In much wisdom is much grief; and he
that acquires knowledge acquires travail and torment."[5]

In such cases the cure may be worse than the disease, and
the victims of medicine are much better off mad—for nothing
now can make commensurable the "intolerable disparity between
the hugeness of their desire and the smallness of reality."[6] This is
why the various exercises for contemplating the body in the body
should not be taken as an isolated or total practice—as some
practitioners do, who contemplate breathing for eight hours a
day over decades. The contemplation of the body in the body
must be balanced with focused meditations on feelings and mental objects, so that we may also see clearly what the love of en-
chantment is, and what joy and grief really are. But feelings and
thoughts are tricky, elusive, complicated; we need to begin our
practice with relatively simple objects of contemplation, such as
breathing—and once we have trained our ability and stamina in
sustained observation, we can move on to subtler contemplations.

---

[5] Montaigne, "Apology for Raymond Sebond," *The Complete
Works*, tr. Donald Frame (Modern Library: New York, 2003) 444).

[6] Simon Leys, "The Imitation of our Lord Don Quixote," *New
York Review of Books*, June 11, 1998.

11. Death like the Sun:
Mindfulness (5)

"I would like to die peacefully in my sleep, like my grandfather—and not screaming in terror like his passengers." The old joke is funny because it is true: most people would prefer not to experience their death and would rather sleep through it, while those who have no choice but to meet it with open eyes go to it screaming with desperate resistance. Yet of the few things that we can have certainty about—besides the facts that you and I are breathing right now, and have bodies—nothing is more certain than that we will die and that we don't know how we will die. If we want to make any sense of our lives, we must surely look first to the meager handful of things we can be certain about, and see what meaning we can draw from them. Strangely, even though after birth, death may be the most important event of our lives, we try our utmost to avoid it and also to avoid thinking about it. Most people do not experience their deaths, and even if they are conscious or in clear enough mind at the time, they are dragged terrified into it and are in no state to be intelligently receptive. *Few people get to know death*, says La Rochefoucauld. *We seldom suffer it from resolution, but from stupidity and habit; and most men die because they cannot help dying.*(*Maxims*, 23)[1] If we do not die quietly in in our sleep, a heart attack or violent accident might also prevent us from the unpleasant witnessing of our own death; or else we die secure in the comfort of a myth of an afterlife in which we do not really die. La Rochefoucauld describes this kind

---

[1] La Rouchefoucauld, *Maxims* (South Bend, Indiana: St. Augustine's Press, 2001) 7.

of comfort as being like the blindfold that prisoners wear before execution. In expiring with our eyes closed or turned away, we miss an essential, even climactic moment—like turning our faces away from a race when the runners are in the last stretch because we can't bear to see it end.

Broodings on death thread through every literate tradition. Most philosophers and poets acknowledge that we cannot develop into full human beings if we are constantly running away from death. When Socrates in Plato's *Phaedo* said that "to philosophize is to learn how to die," what he meant was that in the practice of philosophy we learn to separate our intelligent soul from the unknowable, changing body—but this too strikes me as one of those blindfolds, a refusal to see the mortality of our most cherished part. In an essay actually called "To philosophize is to learn how to die," Montaigne rails against our attempts to ignore death:

> The goal of our career is death. It is the necessary object of our aim. If it frightens us, how is it possible to go a step forward without feverishness? The remedy of the common herd is not to think about it. But from what brutish stupidity can come so gross a blindness![2]

> ...there is no man so decrepit that as long as he sees Methuselah ahead of him, he does not think he has another twenty years left in his body. Furthermore, poor fool that you are, who has assured you the term of your life? You are building on the tales of doctors. Look rather at facts and experience. By the ordinary run of things, you have been

---

[2] Montaigne, "To Philosophize is to Learn How to Die," *The Complete Works*, translated by Donald Frame (New York: Modern Library, 2003) 69.

living a long time now by extraordinary favor. You have passed the accustomed limits of life...[3]

Let us rid it of its strangeness, come to know it, get used to it. Let us have nothing on our minds as often as death. At every moment let us picture it in our imagination in all its aspects...It is uncertain where death awaits us; let us await it everywhere. Premeditation of death is premeditation of freedom. He who has learned how to die has unlearned how to be a slave. Knowing how to die frees us from all subjection and constraint. There is nothing evil in life for the man who has thoroughly grasped the fact that to be deprived of life is not an evil. [4]

We cannot be free if we are afraid of death—practically, because we lock ourselves into lifelong efforts to obtain and guarantee our safety; and philosophically, because terror of death will cause us to espouse views that give us comfort. Montaigne describes his own daily practice to "rob it of its strangeness," which involves remembering all the endlessly surprising ways in which death has arrived and imagining how it might come to him at any moment:

How many ways has death to surprise us!...Who would ever have thought that a duke of Britanny would be stifled to death by a crowd, as that duke was at the entrance of Pope Clement, my neighbor, into Lyons? Haven't you seen one of our kings killed at play? And did not one of his ancestors die from the charge of a hog? Aeschylus, threatened with the fall of a house, takes every precaution --in vain: he gets himself killed by a sort of roof, the shell of a tortoise dropped by a flying eagle. Another dies from a grape seed; an emperor from the scratch of a comb, while combing his hair; Aemilius Lepidus through stumbling against his

---

[3] Ibid., 71.
[4] Ibid., 72.

threshold, and Aufidius through bumping against the door of the council chamber on his way in; and between women's thighs, Cornelius Gallus the praetor, Tigillanus, captain of the watch at Rome, Ludovico, son of Guido de Gonzaga, marquis of Mantua—and still worse, the Platonic philosopher Speusippus, and one of our Popes. Poor Bebius, a judge, in the act of granting a week's postponement to a litigant, has a seizure, his own term of living having expired; and Caius Julius, a doctor, is anointing the eyes of a patient, when along comes death and closes his. And, if I must bring myself into this, a brother of mine, Captain Saint-Martin, twenty-three years old, who had already given pretty good proof of his valor, while playing tennis was struck by a ball a little above the right ear, with no sign of contusion or wound. He did not sit down or rest, but five or six hours later he died of an apoplexy that this blow gave him. With such frequent and ordinary examples passing before our eyes, how can we possibly rid ourselves of the thought of death and of the idea that at every moment it is gripping us by the throat?[5]

Through such musings we can become "intimate" with death, and such intimacy makes us more open to embracing the great philosophical consolations in which our deaths present themselves as good and attractive:

> Your death is a part of the order of the universe; it is a part of the life of the world...Death is the condition of your creation, it is a part of you; you are fleeing from your own selves. This being of yours that you enjoy is equally divided between death and life. The first day of your birth leads you toward death as toward life...[6]

Montaigne's contemplations of death can be read as a kind of

---

[5] Ibid., 71.
[6] Ibid., 78.

Mindfulness practice, in which we engage in focused meditation on our extinction and remember what we are. Yet what he is really doing is riffing playfully on the idea of dying, through a multitude of examples and speculations. I begin this essay with Montaigne because his form of meditation is strikingly different from the Buddha's approach in the *Satipatthana Sutta*. There, in the section on contemplating the body in the body, we are given nine exercises for contemplating a dead body, representing nine phases in decomposition. Montaigne would regard these exercises as a cogent and powerful method to "rid death of its strangeness," but what we notice on first reading of the *Satipatthana* is that the dead person is considered solely *as body*, with attention given only to the physical process of decay. In contrast, Montaigne's consideration of death includes all aspects of the person at once, without differentiation. I will quote all nine exercises together:

> 1. "And further, O bhikkhus, if a bhikkhu, in whatever way, sees a body dead, one, two, or three days: swollen, blue and festering, thrown into the charnel ground, he thinks of his own body thus: 'This body of mine too is of the same nature as that body, is going to be like that body and has not got past the condition of becoming like that body.'

> 2. "And, further, O bhikkhus, if a bhikkhu, in whatever way, sees, whilst it is being eaten by crows, hawks, vultures, dogs, jackals or by different kinds of worms, a body that had been thrown into the charnel ground, he thinks of his own body thus: 'This body of mine, too, is of the same nature as that body, is going to be like that body, and has not got past the condition of becoming like that body.'

> 3. "And, further, O bhikkhus, if a bhikkhu, in whatever way, sees a body, thrown in the charnel ground and reduced to a skeleton together with (some) flesh and blood held in

by the tendons, he thinks of his own body thus: 'This body of mine, too, is of the same nature as that body, is going to be like that body, and has not got past the condition of becoming like that body.'

4."And, further, O bhikkhus, if a bhikkhu, in whatever way, sees a body thrown in the charnel ground and reduced to a blood-besmeared skeleton without flesh but held in by the tendons, he thinks of his own body thus: 'This body of mine, too, is of the same nature as that body, is going to be like that body, and has not got past the condition of becoming like that body.'

5. "And, further, O bhikkhus, if a bhikkhu, in whatever way, sees a body thrown in the charnel ground and reduced to a skeleton held in by the tendons but without flesh and not besmeared with blood, he thinks of his own body thus: 'This body of mind, too, is of the same nature as that body, is going to be like that body, and has not got past the condition of becoming like that body.'

6. "And, further, O bhikkhus, if a bhikkhu, in whatever way, sees a body thrown in the charnel ground and reduced to bones gone loose, scattered in all directions — a bone of the hand, a bone of the foot, a shin bone, a thigh bone, the pelvis, spine and skull, each in a different place — he thinks of his own body thus: 'This body of mine, too, is of the same nature as that body, is going to be like that body, and has not got past the condition of becoming like that body.'

7."And, further, O bhikkhus, if a bhikkhu, in whatever way, sees a body thrown in the charnel ground and reduced to bones, white in color like a conch, he thinks of his own body thus: 'This body of mine, too, is of the same nature as that body, going to be like that body and has not got past the condition of becoming like that body:'

8. "And, further, O bhikkhus, if a bhikkhu, in whatever way, sees a body thrown in the charnel ground and reduced to bones more than a year old, heaped together, he thinks of his own body thus: 'This body of mine, too, is of the same nature as that body, is going to be like that body and has not got past the condition of becoming like that body.'

9. "And, further, O bhikkhus, if a bhikkhu, in whatever way, sees a body thrown in the charnel ground and reduced to bones gone rotten and become dust, he thinks of his own body thus: 'This body of mine too, is of the same nature as that body, is going to be like that body and has not got past the condition of becoming like that body.'"[7]

We are asked to look, to see, to pay attention to decay, disintegration, and dispersal as phases in an inevitable process. This is all the more necessary in a society such as ours, where we are systematically shielded from dying and death, and where natural decay is concealed from us by the funeral industry. In a culture that fetishizes youth and depends for its continuation on the feeding of an infinite collective appetite, we do not get to see decay; we barely even get to see people bent over in advanced age. The closest most of us get to decay is roadkill, but we never stop to look because by definition we are on the road speeding by the kill. Perhaps we should stop to look, since it will be one of our few opportunities to witness decay for ourselves. With modern scientific instruments, we can also see that putrefaction is a wonderfully complex and ordered process, with laws and patterns. Even with our naked eyes it is possible to watch the corpse becoming billions of beings, many of which came from within it anyway and lived as part of it. We witness how the body is not one thing, and its multifarious motion in death reflects also its

---

[7] Soma Thera.

84

manifoldness in life—and how determined by conditions each phase is! There are not really even phases, only a continuous process until the body has returned to its elements, which in turn partake in other processes that might result in new bodies. Daily observation of these transformations eventually wears away our squeamishness in the face of decay, making us capable of living with death and disintegration as they go on all around us.

That is one part of the meditation. The other part is the refrain, *'This body of mine, too, is of the same nature as that body, is going to be like that body and has not got past the condition of becoming like that body.'* My body is the same as this corpse and has not managed to transcend the conditions of dying and decay. Notice that the Buddha does not say "I am of the same nature as this body": he is not reducing the whole human being to its physical processes, and is focusing here only on the body. The refrain has to be more than a mere verbal acknowledgment; when we say it and mean it, what we are expressing is a growing acquaintance with the natural processes as we are experiencing them right now in *this* body that grows old and will die. In my 50s, I can know in every aspect of the body that the processes of dying and decay are happening in me, albeit—so far—less dramatically than in the corpse, and it is all an integral aspect of being alive in flux. Without this same flux I would never have been born and would never have grown to maturity: nothing would have happened. Even though these thoughts are going beyond contemplating the body in the body, they flow naturally from recognizing myself in the corpse before me and are a consequence of remembering what I am. At the end of each of these exercises the Buddha repeats the encouragement to reflect in a rounded way on what we have discovered through observation:

> Thus he lives contemplating the body in the body internally, or he lives contemplating the body in the body externally, or he lives contemplating the body in the body internally

and externally. He lives contemplating origination-things in the body, or he lives contemplating dissolution-things in the body, or he lives contemplating origination-and-dissolution-things in the body. Or his mindfulness is established with the thought, 'The body exists,' to the extent necessary just for knowledge and remembrance, and he lives independent and clings to naught in the world."

The regular undertaking of this exercise changes us, making us more open and attuned to the vibrant, perilous buzz of the organic world around us and in us—and no longer afraid of it all. Our mindfulness is established with the thought, 'The body exists': this is what it is for body to be body, there is no other way for body to be and consequently no way for any of us to escape from this condition. However, the simple recognition that this is how things are can easily be elevated into a grand, dark theory of life. Therefore we are mindful *to the extent necessary for knowledge and remembrance,* and should catch ourselves sliding into morbidity, transcendentalism, or any view that would replace and cover up the raw experience. This is why the Buddha calls for contemplating a corpse—not contemplating death or dying. A corpse is an observable fact, and our identification with it is grounded in experience—whereas "death" and "dying" are conceptions from the point of view of a consciousness that is clinging to the supposed opposite of these conceptions. Without an attachment to "life," death is not an opposite that has to be neutralized; instead, there is only a process of transformation, moment by moment.

La Rochefoucauld remarks cryptically, *Neither the sun nor death can be looked at fixedly* (*Maxims*, 26, author's translation).[8] Just as we cannot stare directly at the sun without squinting or getting blinded, so we cannot take a direct look at death. In the corpse contemplations the bhikkhu doesn't even try to look at

---

[8] La Rochefoucauld, *Maxims*, 26.

"death" or "dying," focusing instead only on the body and eliminating from the picture the rest of the being that is conceived as dying. The effect is not any theory about death, but the removal of an obstruction to experiencing the entire process that is meant by the word "death."

12. Learning from Feelings: Mindfulness (6)

Feelings, Nothing More Than Feelings... —Morris Albert

Are you the same as your body? After a period of time cultivating focused awareness of breathing, postures, movements, and decay, it is tempting to conclude that we are not the same as our bodies—and that the witnessing consciousness stands above and outside of the ceaseless flux of embodied life. The contemplations of the body in the body are perfectly compatible with philosophies that view the essential self as bodiless—as the impersonal intellect, or as the individual soul, or as Spirit opposed to Matter, or as the universal Self or Atman that forms the eternal substratum to the changing world. For all such philosophies, the contemplation of the body in the body would be a highly effective way to wean us from identifying with the body and instead teach us to identify with the unchanging part of ourselves. But are we only twofold—an eternal something inhabiting a changing, material body? Certainly the eternal something cannot be found apart from body, but is the part of us that is not body simply an eternal soul, or are there aspects and gradations to it? In the *Satipatthana Sutta*, the Buddha goes from body to feelings:

> And how, O bhikkhus, does a bhikkhu live contemplating feeling in feelings?[1]

Before going on, I should point put that the English word *feelings* misses the mark. The word translated is *vedana*, which is

---

[1] Soma Thera.

not "feelings" as in "emotions." The latter tends to come in a complex package that is made up of both affect and thought. In fact, all emotions come from thought on some level and cannot be separated from it—for instance, anger is usually an emotion that issues from some perception of injustice, and love is inextricably tied to some thought of the good and the beautiful. When we hate someone, it is because we think they are bad; indeed, whenever we despise or admire someone, our feelings flow from conscious evaluation. With normal *emotions*, we cannot contemplate *feelings in feelings*, stripped away from other aspects of mental life.

The Buddha—in his penetrating observation of everything that goes on inside a person—drew into the foreground one level of our experience that usually goes unnoticed and undiscussed. We have six sense faculties that are made to sense six kinds of things. (For Buddhists as for Hindus, the sixth sense is the mind, which is both the internal sense organ and also the sense that brings together the perceptions of the other senses, as when we realize that the orange object sensed by our eyes, the sweet but tart object sensed by our taste, and the spherical object sensed by our touch, are in fact aspects of one thing, namely an orange.) When we sense something, there is a perception, but there is always simultaneously a feeling *tone* to that perception. To take an analogy: a cook makes a dish for the king, gives it a taste-test, and, with some trepidation, finds it acceptable; the king just tastes it and enjoys it. Both cook and king might have the same taste-perception of the dish, but their reactions on tasting are what the Buddha is calling *vedana* or "feelings." Clearly, the *vedana* and the taste-perception are not separate, but they are distinct. If the cook makes the identical dish every day, after a week the king might have the same taste-perception of this dish, but the feeling may have turned to dislike. Thus, while feeling and perception come together, the specific feeling is not intrinsic to the perception. Another strange fact regarding *vedana* is that with any given sense perception we usually cannot help feeling what we feel, and what we feel can often surprise us.

The observation that there is such a dimension to experience as *vedana* is both original and profoundly important in the Buddha's path out of suffering. Feelings lead to craving, and craving leads to attachment—and once we are attached, we are committed to suffering. To give an example that I will amplify in a later essay: I am handed a bowl of ice-cream of a flavor new to me, I taste it (sense perception), I like it (feeling), I want more (craving), I want a second bowl (more craving), and I need to find out where I can buy it so that it is either always in my fridge or permanently available to me (attachment). In attachment we attempt to guarantee the object for ourselves, and the money we pay for the ice-cream goes towards securing the future production of it as well as the means of delivery—in other words, we *make* the world that guarantees us this ice-cream. Once we get to this point we are committed, shackled, and any disturbance of this security makes us unhappy. The same sequence of feeling-craving-attachment can be experienced in all our commitments: reading, career, friendship, romance, religions, philosophies. I experienced this, I liked it, I wanted more, I tried to secure it. In the suttas on craving, the Buddha asks us to notice that the chain starts with the link from feeling to craving, but that craving is not intrinsic to feeling: it is possible to be perfectly content with one taste of ice-cream, and indeed to enjoy it more that way. But the problem is that usually tasting, feeling, craving, and attachment all seem to happen simultaneously, "naturally," in one thought. I can't help liking this new ice-cream, but liking it "naturally" seems to mean that I must have it always. In mindfulness meditation, we slow down the apparently natural process and notice that tasting, feeling, craving, and attachment are each discrete. We can't stop ourselves from perceiving, and we can't stop the immediate feeling-reaction to the perception, but we can see that there is a chasm between feeling and craving.

This is why the contemplation of feelings in feeling is so important: if we are to work on craving and attachment, we have to be attentive to the presence of *vedana* all the time. The actual exercise of contemplating feelings in feeling in the *Satipatthana* is relatively short, less than a page, but it is an extremely fertile and demanding exercise. The exercises on body are much more extensive and varied, because they are training-wheels, as it were. Mindfulness of breathing and movements, while good practices in themselves, also enable us to cultivate powers of observation, sensitivity, and stamina with relatively obvious objects—whereas feelings and thoughts are more volatile and elusive. If you can't do the exercise on breathing, the one on feelings will be far out of your reach. In what follows, the Buddha works with only three categories of *vedana*—pleasant, unpleasant, and indifferent or not-sure—and with two levels of them, to do with gross physical sensation and mental or imaginative sensation:

> "Here, O bhikkhus, a bhikkhu when experiencing a pleasant feeling, understands: 'I experience a pleasant feeling'; when experiencing a painful feeling, he understands: 'I experience a painful feeling'; when experiencing a neither-pleasant-nor-painful feeling, he understands: 'I experience a neither-pleasant-nor-painful feeling'; when experiencing a pleasant worldly feeling, he understands: 'I experience a pleasant worldly feeling'; when experiencing a pleasant spiritual feeling, he understands: 'I experience a pleasant spiritual feeling'; when experiencing a painful worldly feeling, he understands: 'I experience a painful worldly feeling'; when experiencing a painful spiritual feeling, he understands: 'I experience a painful spiritual feeling'; when experiencing a neither-pleasant-nor-painful worldly feeling, he understands: 'I experience a neither-pleasant-nor-painful worldly feeling'; when experiencing a neither-pleasant-nor-

painful spiritual feeling, he understands: 'I experience a nei-
ther-pleasant-nor-painful spiritual feeling.'"[2]

At first these categories seem too simple to be true, as if we
were labeling each *vedana* with a crude emoticon. But the Buddha's project here is to simplify, to pare the vedanas down to the
barest and most undeniable characteristic of *like, don't like,* or *not
sure.* More sophisticated emotional overtones, such as "fascinating" and "sad," are harder to nail down because they have so
many thought-shadings and associations, and because they
change so quickly and, indeed, wobble. The category of neither-
pleasant-nor-painful is particularly interesting, because often it
exists *because* of the other two: if you tend to like and dislike pas-
sionately, the extremes will create a neutral middle-ground that
we mostly experience as "uninteresting" or "boring." The phenomenon of a "boring life" is the artifact of an excessive attachment to what we "like" and "dislike," an attachment that has
somehow sprung from the initial feelings of liking and disliking.
When we pay attention to those feelings as they arise, watch
them in their courses, and notice that they do actually diminish,
we will be much less prone to just letting them turn to cravings.

We all know that the more we observe, the more we find
there is to observe. When we started on mindfulness of breathing, it didn't seem that there would be much to it, but as we become more perceptive, we start to find the act of breathing, in
the whole body, infinitely interesting. The objects of sense perception are overwhelming in their multitude. As I sit here, if I
pause my writing, I can notice all six of my senses going at one
moment or another, and each distinct sense perception is accompanied by a *vedana.* There are hundreds in a minute. It is an ath-
letic feat to keep up with them all, and the effect of even short
bursts of contemplating feelings can be like a deafening, blinding

---

[2] Soma Thera.

bombardment of stimuli both from inside and outside. In one of the Buddha's similes, we are compared to a flayed cow standing in a field, exposed to millions of stinging insects and the assaults of weather. In this exercise, we realize vividly how much there is going on in our experience all the time, and how easily we latch onto some things and feverishly shun other things. In this buzzing jungle of feelings, attachments—especially as attractions and aversions—form rapidly and then take on lives of their own that grow into monsters that consume us. But here we nip the attachments in the bud by just watching the feelings and letting them be: they arise, grow, dwindle, and vanish, equal in status, none of them getting preferential treatment, and none of them outcast. We do not know where they come from, why they came, or where they go to: we are not the authors of them.

The Buddha then gives the reflective refrain:

> Thus he lives contemplating feelings in feelings internally, or he lives contemplating feelings in feelings externally, or he lives contemplating feelings in feelings internally and externally. He lives contemplating origination-things in feelings, or he lives contemplating dissolution-things in feelings, or he lives contemplating origination-and-dissolution-things in feelings. Or his mindfulness is established with the thought: 'Feeling exists,' to the extent necessary just for knowledge and remembrance and he lives independent and clings to naught in the world."[3]

Having chewed on this paragraph after each of the exercises in contemplating body, we start to hear some of the familiar words with new ears. The bhikkhu *lives* contemplating in this way: it is not merely an exercise. And with feelings, we can become acutely aware of origination and dissolution, as well as both together. Nothing stays still. It is in the nature of feeling to be

---

[3] Soma Thera.

this way; indeed, there is no other way for feeling to be! When we want to secure unending access to the marvelous ice-cream, what we are trying to do is to repeat the pleasure of the first taste—to repeat it forever. But this is not in the nature of feelings, for no two spoonfuls of the ice-cream will result in the same feeling: if we attempt to repeat, we will be disappointed—and in our intense expectation of a repeat, we will block ourselves from experiencing something new. Yet "feeling exists": there is no way, if we have sense perception, that it will not exist. We acknowledge it, and remember to heed the warning not to get carried away by our experience in meditation to make more of the ephemerality of feeling than it really is—for instance, not to elevate it into an aesthetic in which we strain to develop a sentimental, nostalgic relationship to the moment, as with much classical Japanese literature. We practice mindfulness *to the extent necessary just for knowledge and remembrance,* and certainly not for the pleasant feelings it might cause in us.

If we want to believe that the experiencing consciousness is separate from and transcends the world of the body, we can—with the Cartesians—think of sense-perception and *vedanas* as being essentially of the body, because they are both in and of the kingdom of flux. But *vedanas* are interesting and problematic, because they shade into volitions and commitments; and, since there indubitably exist feelings of pleasure and pain accompanying mental objects of perception—ideas, thoughts, images, dreams—the *vedanas* have to be considered an aspect of the very consciousness that is experiencing the objects of the six senses. Even the least worldly person has *vedana* towards geometry, a Bach partita, the idea of God, the mystery of death. It is much harder, after undertaking the contemplation of feelings in feeling, to take refuge in the thought that "I" am the unchanging, untouched, witnessing consciousness standing aloof from the mutable world of matter.

13. Knowing Our Own Minds: Mindfulness (7)

For a philosophy that systematically raises doubts about the reality of the individual soul, it is surprising that so much Buddhist literature consists of accounts of meetings between a particular teacher and a particular student. The Pali Nikayas are filled with thousands of pages of conversations between the Buddha and various disciples, kings, or Brahmin visitors; and the classical Zen *koan* is an encounter of two people, in which one of them suddenly "sees" or doesn't see. We, the readers of these, are encountering the encounter, meeting the meeting of minds.

When two minds "meet," the first thing that happens before anything is said is that one has to get the measure of the other: who am I dealing with, what kind of person, what kind of intelligence? This also applies to competitive tournaments—chess, fencing, wrestling, pingpong—where you find yourself facing someone you have never met before; and you don't always have much time to figure out who you are dealing with and how you are going to beat him. The gauging of the other mind has to happen very quickly, and it demands powers of accurate intuition. Even if you are acquainted with the other person, you still don't know how they are *today*; something big might have happened since yesterday. This is of course true with every interaction. In conversations, if neither interlocutor is good at guessing the state of the other person's mind, the two of them are likely to talk at cross-purposes and fail to "meet" in any fruitful way. This is most true of teaching situations. A good teacher has to have a developed intuition for "where" her student is, and this "where" is not determined only by tests that give numerical scores for knowledge and skills. The more important conditions for learning have to do with disposition, attitude, and character: how distracted or agitated is the student today, is there anything else weighing on his mind, can he concentrate fully or think clearly, did he get enough sleep, is he hungry, is he angry, is he having girlfriend problems or serious issues in his home life, has he developed sufficient strength of character to pull himself together for today's lesson? Such issues are significant conditions for learning or not learning, and if the teacher ignores them or has no capacity to notice them, very little learning will occur. Unfortunately, many educational systems today reduce success or failure to quantifiable results, and are completely ignorant of the more important, unquantifiable dimensions of the teacher's art.

A skillful teacher therefore has to be minutely aware of the students' "state of mind," for want of a better phrase. In the Pali Discourses of the Buddha, my phrase "state of mind" translates *citta*, which is also rendered in different translations as "mind" or "consciousness." Just as teaching requires mindfulness of *citta*, so does self-cultivation—which is the primary form of learning for adults, who should be mature enough to steer themselves. But we can only steer ourselves if we know "where" we are. Thus, an adult who decides to develop the characteristics of warrior nobility cannot simply decide to have integrity, courage, justice, wisdom, and invincible fighting skills. Each one of these is developed through baby steps, and before we embark on a program of training we first have to know where to begin and exactly how far away we are from our goals. For the same reasons, once we have begun, we need to be able to evaluate where we are at every step.

This is why the third Foundation of Mindfulness in the *Satipatthana Sutta* is contemplating consciousness [*citta*] in consciousness:

> And how, O bhikkhus, does a bhikkhu live contemplating consciousness in consciousness?[1]

In martial arts training, lapses in attention and malfunctions in thinking are manifested physically, making it easy for the opponent or the sensei to administer a sharp corrective. In meditation, we are mostly on our own, and when we are attempting to find our way through the confusion of our own thoughts and emotions—many of which are only dimly glimpsed—we need to be able to take our own measure. The Buddha, in the formulaic style favored by his Pali editors, gives us a checklist of things to examine, which I take to be not rigid prescriptions but strong recommendations, leaving us free to modify it appropriately for our own needs:

> Here, O bhikkhus, a bhikkhu understands the consciousness with lust, as with lust; the consciousness without lust, as without lust; the consciousness with hate, as with hate; the consciousness without hate, as without hate; the consciousness with ignorance, as with ignorance; the consciousness without ignorance, as without ignorance; the shrunken state of consciousness, as the shrunken state; the distracted state of consciousness, as the distracted state; the state of consciousness become great, as the state become great; the state of consciousness not become great, as the state not become great; the state of consciousness with some other mental state superior to it, as the state with something mentally higher; the state of consciousness with no other mental state superior to it, as the state with nothing mentally higher; the quieted state of consciousness, as

---

[1] Soma Thera.

the quieted state; the state of consciousness not quieted, as the state not quieted; the freed state of consciousness as freed; and the unfreed state of consciousness, as unfreed."[2]

These are the kinds of consideration undertaken by any good teacher regarding her students—because there is no point giving them assignments that they are not mentally or emotionally prepared to do. What is particularly moving in texts like the *Satipatthana* is that we are expected to be able to do this ourselves. Indeed, no one else can do it for us. At almost every stage of the training, the student is asked to self-reflect and to review. If there is the will to progress, the capacity to evaluate and investigate can always be refined. Because our "state of mind" determines what we are capable of doing at any given time, we need to be aware, as we practice, of our current *citta* and how it might be changing. As with bodily phenomena and feelings, we notice that different states arise and then subside; they never stay the same, and they can be affected through training. It is a little bit like sailing a boat on a vast, dark ocean: we cannot necessarily change the ocean at any given time, but we can become minutely aware of winds and waters, and learn to navigate with skill to our destination.

This ideal is very difficult to achieve, because *citta* is a subtler, more pervasive object of contemplation than neither body or feelings. If you remember a time when you spent hours trying to reason with someone consumed with anger, you will also remember feeling frustrated and hopeless because your interlocutor was so submerged in anger that there was no way he could hear anything else: calm reasoning was futile. The problem with *citta* is that we identify with our mind-states, we believe them, we see through them. This is why some translators render *citta* as "consciousness": our *citta* is nothing less than how we see things at

---

[2] Soma Thera.

any moment, and consciousness is always manifest in the form of some *citta*. We never find pure consciousness without *citta*, just as we never find it without body or without feelings. Thus, your angry interlocutor had consciousness with anger, and you had a dismayed state of *consciousness with some other mental state superior to it,* to use the Buddha's formula. At the time of your argument, you couldn't realize that your angry interlocutor was equally frustrated with your inability to see the full justice of his fury. *Citta* is of the nature of passion, in that we are largely passive to it—and when we are deep in passion, it is very hard to see our own *citta* objectively. We identify with our passions. This is why when we are challenged in our *citta*, we tend to get angry or defensive—because we feel that it is we ourselves who are being attacked. To be mindful of our own *citta*, as a skilled teacher is mindful of the *citta* of her student, is to have attained a very high order of mindfulness. At this point the philosophical dualist would still say, Is the consciousness of *citta* the same kind of thing as *citta*, or is it not necessarily transcendent to it? The Buddha would reply, Can you point to it independently of the *citta* it is conscious of? The observing consciousness is still *citta*, still conditioned—and it will change, conditioned by its next set of determinants.

The contemplation of *citta* reaches very deeply into the question of who we are. Now, when we get the Buddha's reflective refrain—which by this time we know by heart—we hear some new insights:

> Thus he lives contemplating consciousness in consciousness internally, or he lives contemplating consciousness in consciousness externally, or he lives contemplating consciousness in consciousness internally and externally. He lives contemplating origination-things in consciousness, or he lives contemplating dissolution-things in consciousness, or he lives contemplating origination-and-dissolution-things in consciousness. Or his mindfulness is established with the

thought: 'Consciousness exists,' to the extent necessary just for knowledge and remembrance, and he lives independent and clings to naught in the world.[3]

States of mind have originations and dissolutions. Like corporeal sensations and the *vedanas*, nothing stays still from one moment to another; only the practice of careful, focused contemplation will teach us to be sensitive to even the minutest flickerings of change. *Consciousness exists*: this is how it is, there is no other way for consciousness to be, no place to go for it to become permanent. The Buddha's matter-of-fact approach is especially valuable in this kind of meditation, for we are prone to take its objects personally and become upset and resistant. For example, if we find in ourselves a *citta* of laziness and if we happen to be the kind of person who flees laziness at all cost, our immediate reaction will tend to be disgust with ourselves and the desire to change—which of course is another *citta*, so we would be automatically flying from one state to another. The Buddha tells us just to contemplate, not to struggle; let it be, find it interesting, and let it pass—because it will pass. We contemplate not for the sake of fixing ourselves or to make ourselves perfect, but *to the extent necessary just for knowledge and remembrance*. Knowing that states of *citta* are as fleeting and insubstantial as bodily motions and feelings—insubstantial in the sense that there is no unchanging substance underlying them to give them fixity and solidity—the student does not cling to *citta* as a refuge that transcends all change.

One practical benefit to this way of engaging with states of mind is that in accepting the various states as they occur in our own beings, we become generally more relaxed and understanding when they manifest themselves in other people: the perceived stupidity and obstinacy of the other party is no more identified

---

[3] Soma Thera.

with them as our wisdom and righteousness are identified with us. Thus the advanced practitioner lives, contemplating *citta* in *citta*, internally and externally.

14. The Buddha's Core Curriculum for Graduating Life: Mindfulness (8)

If the *Satipatthana Sutta* were to conclude after describing the first three foundations of mindfulness, what would we lose? Mindfulness of breathing, bodily movements and positions, feelings, and states of mind will be more than enough for most people to work on over several decades and still feel they haven't exhausted the practice. We would gain closeness to our own experience: a refined awareness of all that is going on in our bodies, an understanding of how feelings work and how craving arises, a developed intuition for states of mind in ourselves and in others, a diminishing of compulsions and attachments, and all round—just by becoming more aware and self-aware—greater effectiveness in our activities. Becoming more open to experience and more calmly intelligent about what really goes on, we will naturally suffer less because our expectations and demands will be more realistic; we might even find ourselves happier, because we are struggling less with people and situations, and because in paying attention we will start to find our own lives more interesting, more abundant. It could well be that knowledge of what we have to do and how we have to live will emerge naturally from understanding ourselves better—just as children who read and who thus spend many hours a day getting into the minds of literary characters will expand their powers of empathy without having to be taught.

The Buddha himself made his great spiritual discoveries wholly empirically, through observing and comprehending what is present in body, feelings, and mind; no one told him where the practice was going to lead him. It takes tremendous trust in the process to be able to give oneself up to the lessons of experience, without being guided by a framework reassuringly provided by a wise teacher. Similarly, it takes an unusually trusting teacher to let the student loose in the laboratory of life to figure out for himself what works and what doesn't. What if the student accidentally blows himself up? On the other hand, a real teacher—knowing that he is not omniscient—is always delighted when a student surprises him with a question or discovery that he hasn't yet thought of. Throughout the Discourses the Buddha has emphasized "knowing for yourselves"; we only know the things that we find with our own senses and intelligence, and the Buddha's teaching style—terse, dry, understated—is designed to give us space to question and investigate. It is also why the *Satipatthana* starts with meditations in which we develop confidence in our own powers of insight. In the words of the refrain in this Sutta, the practitioner "lives independent and clings to naught in the world"—not even the words of his teacher. In the cultivation if mindfulness, the Buddha is scrupulous not to introduce the conceptual frame too early, for premature reliance on someone else's interpretation of phenomena always undermines our own ability to experience honestly.

Only as the fourth foundation of mindfulness do we start contemplating the *dhammas*—often confusingly translated "mental objects," because it deals with ideas and emotions, and consists of a series of formulaic encapsulations of the Buddha's system that need to be considered and understood. To oversimplify, the first three foundations of mindfulness cultivate accurate but passive awareness, a kind of wise receptivity to what is; by themselves, they have little power of active transformation, little capacity to take us further along the path that leads to the final destruction of suffering. In the first three mindfulness practices, we ward nothing away, repress nothing, and entertain with open arms both positive and negative equally; in the fourth mindful-ness practice, we must now work to nudge away the negative and develop the positive, since we now understand vividly what nega-tive and positive are.

The martial sport of fencing offers a useful analogy. A bud-ding fencer might be fond of swords, and while using the finest sports blades he might be thinking all the time of his home col-lection of beautifully crafted antique rapiers: mindfulness of the blade, an intimate knowledge of everything about swords, moti-vates and excites this student's practice. Another fencer might be on fire from the historical romance of fencing, and in each prac-tice session he remembers real duels and the accounts of ancient combats. A third fencer, perhaps coming from a background in dance or gymnastics, might enjoy the technical drills more, and appreciate the science of movement: here we see a certain kind of mindfulness of body. None of these interests is wrong, and each of them brings into the foreground one aspect of the sport. The aspect that is foregrounded may be in itself endlessly fascinating and rewarding, but the fencer who is "lost" in a single aspect will not become a good fencer. What is required in the making of a real fencer is the harnessing of a host of subordinate aspects into the ability to win bouts against skilled antagonists, and this in-volves progressions of learning directed towards a specific end. The training is vigorous and prescriptive—do this, don't do that—as the student is actively transformed into a real fencer who might survive in an actual sword fight.

The contemplation of *dhammas* ("mental objects") takes place in accordance with five numerical frames that are given more detailed treatment in other Suttas: the five hindrances, the five aggregates of clinging, the six internal and external sense bases, the seven factors of enlightenment, and the four noble truths. Each of these is a concise, standard schema of ethical, intellectual, and psychological soul-work; they are compressions of the Buddha's experience that need to be carefully considered and unpacked for ourselves—like seeds of wisdom, which grow only if watered, by our own hands, with our blood. The first three foundations of mindfulness were necessary propaedeutics to this, for without developed attentiveness to our own experience the contemplation of *dhammas* would be entirely out of our reach. The Four Noble Truths make only superficial, hypothetical sense to one who does not know how to be mindful of body and feelings. Indeed, many people who are suffering believe that they are fine, and many who think they are suffering badly are in fact better off than most—how would we know how to recognize and gauge our own state, if our powers of awareness are nothing more than rudimentary and blunt, like sticks that small boys use as pretend-weapons?

I am not going to investigate all the contemplations of *dhammas* here, because they require longer and more detailed consideration and because I am unqualified. Whereas the first three foundations make a lot of sense to me, the fourth requires trust and commitment to the Buddha's system—trust and commitment that is backed up by seeing, in the practice of the first three foundations, that the Buddha always has a reason for saying what he says in the way he says it. The contemplation of *dhammas* is for students who have already committed to the path, but here too the articulations make sense to an ordinary thoughtful human being who seeks to be wiser.

For example, one of the contemplations of *dhammas* takes on the "five hindrances" (*nivarana*), those complexes of thoughts and emotions that interrupt and obstruct our efforts at mental clarity and tranquillity in whatever work we may be doing. They are difficult to deal with, because by the time we become aware of the presence of one of them, our work has already been disturbed. Because our foundations in mindfulness are now strong, we can nonetheless pull back and look at the disturbance.

"Here, O bhikkhus, a bhikkhu lives contemplating the mental objects in the mental objects of the five hindrances. "How, O bhikkhus, does a bhikkhu live contemplating mental objects in the mental objects of the five hindrances? "Here, O bhikkhus, when sensuality is present, a bhikkhu knows with understanding: 'I have sensuality,' or when sensuality is not present, he knows with understanding: 'I have no sensuality.' He understands how the arising of the non-arisen sensuality comes to be; he understands how the abandoning of the arisen sensuality comes to be; and he understands how the non-arising in the future of the abandoned sensuality comes to be. When anger is present, he knows with understanding: 'I have anger,' or when anger is not present, he knows with understanding: 'I have no anger.' He understands how the arising of the non-arisen anger comes to be; he understands how the abandoning of the arisen anger comes to be; and he understands how the non-arising in the future of the abandoned anger comes to be. When sloth and torpor are present, he knows with understanding: 'I have sloth and torpor,' or when sloth and torpor are not present, he knows with understanding: 'I have no sloth and torpor.' He understands how the arising of non-arisen sloth and torpor comes to be; he understands how the abandoning of the arisen sloth and torpor comes to be; and he understands how the non-arising in the future of the abandoned sloth and torpor comes to be. When agitation and worry are present, he knows with understanding: 'I have agitation and worry,' or when agitation and worry are not present, he knows with understanding: 'I have no agitation and worry.' He understands how the arising of non-arisen agitation and worry comes to be; and he understands how the abandoning of the arisen agitation and worry comes to be; and he understands how the non-arising in the future of the abandoned agitation and worry comes to be. When doubt is present, he knows with understanding: 'I have doubt,' or when doubt is not present, he knows with

understanding: 'I have no doubt.' He understands how the
arising of non-arisen doubt comes to be; he understands
how the abandoning of the arisen doubt comes to be; and
he understands how the non-arising in the future of the
abandoned doubt comes to be."[1]

Each of these hindrances hides a world of complex causation. "Sensuality" is not just sexual desire, but all those desires
that come from an underlying belief that material pleasures can
make us happy; "anger" expresses disappointment, dissatisfaction, and a sense of betrayal, stemming from some belief that
people and the world "should" be other than they are, and from a
concealed assumption that we are competent to judge their inad-
equacy; "sloth and torpor" encompass our various ways of resist-
ing what we know we must do, ranging from not being able to
get up or to stay awake, to seeking distraction in trivial entertainments, to depressive paralysis; "agitation and worry," which
can creep in insidiously at any moment, can come from regret for
things done, not done, or done poorly, as well as the anxiety that
is generated by the knowledge of unfinished business, and general anxiety for loved ones and the world; and "doubt," which is
not just lack of faith in the Buddha's path, includes philosophical
mistrust as well as crippling lack of confidence in one's own
abilities and in the project as a whole. The Buddha has seen
clearly—in himself and in his students—that whenever we find
ourselves unsettled and derailed, it is usually because of one or
more of these five hindrances. We also know from experience
that the hindrances are addictive by nature: each time we indulge
them, we make them stronger and more frequent in the future.
Consequently, learning how to handle the hindrances is crucial
to progress along the path, and mindfulness of the hindrances

---

[1] Soma Thera.

comes under the category of *contemplating the dhammas in the dhammas*. While good, encouraging advice from a teacher and close friends is usually our best help in dealing with the hindrances once they have arisen and once we find ourselves wriggling in their clutches, we still have to learn to manage them ourselves by experiencing them directly and seeing what they are.

Let's look at just one of them: *When anger is present, he knows with understanding: 'I have anger,' or when anger is not present, he knows with understanding: 'I have no anger.'* The first step is to be able to recognize when it is there or not there. Often we can go for days in a bad mood without consciously realizing that we are angry; or we can find in the midst of our meditations that we are being swept along on a flash flood of grumbling, not having noticed when it started. This part of the contemplation requires skill in bare mindfulness. But what do we do, once we have noticed? *He understands how the arising of the non-arisen anger comes to be; he understands how the abandoning of the arisen anger comes to be; and he understands how the non-arising in the future of the abandoned anger comes to be.* We have to study where the anger comes from, and be able to recognize it at its origination as it arises—and not only when it has already become full-fledged passion. Once we understand how it arises, we need to understand how it is abandoned. As in the other contemplations, we do not repress or force the hindrance out—because that will only give it more power. Sometimes seeing, hearing, and understanding are sufficient to calm an emotion, but most often we have to learn how to divert or sublimate a thought that might grow into a hindrance. For example, when we are angry with a person, we might go straight to them and talk; or we might try putting ourselves in their shoes. When we have grasped this, we will be in a better position to understand how to live in such a way that anger never just arises. This work involves dedicated self-reflection, awareness of our emotions, and creative intelligence with regard to our toughest, trickiest mental tendencies.

Notice, too, how impersonal the Buddha's phrasing is: *when anger is present*, not *when he is angry*. No one "owns" the anger or "is" the anger; rather, anger is carried by an inertia that we surely contributed to but that we are not sole agents of. For this reason, the hindrance can be calmly worked on, as a sculptor works on granite, and there is no extraneous emotion of blame or resistance that comes from disliking "being like this." The first three foundations of mindfulness have trained us to find this work interesting and productive, and we can now approach the work like skilled craftsmen. One other benefit of this serene engagement is that we will find that other people no longer irk us much, and because we understand the hindrances in ourselves, we are likely to be more understanding and compassionate towards the hindrances as they appear in others.

The *Satipatthana Sutta*, in about 20 pages, gives us a complete curriculum for what can truly be called self-study, with the aim of understanding the origin of suffering and how to end it. Each of the four foundations of mindfulness requires dedicated, concentrated practice, and if we consider how difficult it is to be mindful of only breathing for a single hour, we will have a clear picture of how accomplished we would have to be to sustain mindfulness in all four dimensions for a whole week. *But should any person maintain these Four Arousings of Mindfulness in this manner for a week, then by him one of two fruitions is proper to be expected: Knowledge here and now; or, if some form of clinging is yet present, the state of non-returning.*[2] In purely secular terms, it is possible to see how even a little time devoted every day to these meditative exercises will result in a happier, more effective human being, capable of helping himself and others, and more directly attuned to his own experience. The curriculum laid out in

---

[2] Soma Thera.

the *Satipatthana* may well be, as the Buddha claims, the *one* path to self-knowledge and happiness.

15. What Is the Role of Thinking?

One remarkable feature of spiritual practice today in both East and West is widespread anti-intellectualism: thoughts are only creations "of the mind" and have nothing to do with the things that really matter, so one must "let go" of the mind and find ways to still the thinking process. Obviously --so goes the dogma—it is futile to think about or verbally express God, the Dao, and Enlightenment. Doubting and skepticism are only the mind's wheels cranking away, and the generating of questions and opinions is simply what the mind does, automatically. One hears this in dojos, ashrams, and churches all over the world. This version of anti-intellectualism is cognate with the normal moral and political anti-intellectualism we encounter every day: *We don't need any of your learning or evidence, you're just scholars unnecessarily complicating things that are simple and obvious, you think you're so smart, just find a guru or a successful businessman and do what he says*...In all cases, vehement anti-intellectualism results in obedience to strong leaders and in social cohesion obtained through the nourishing of passions like fear and anger.

Occasionally in the Pali Suttas the Buddha comes across as anti-intellectual. He can seem dismissive of speculative activity and uninterested in philosophical "big questions"—but does he in fact believe that thinking is in itself worthless? In the *Majjhima Nikaya*, we meet the earnest monk Malunkyaputta, who suddenly finds himself stirred up and riled by metaphysical questions:

> I have heard that on one occasion the Blessed One was staying near Savatthi at Jeta's Grove, Anathapindika's monastery. Then, as Ven. Malunkyaputta was alone in seclu-

sion, this train of thought arose in his awareness: "These positions that are undeclared, set aside, discarded by the Blessed One — 'The cosmos is eternal,' 'The cosmos is not eternal,' 'The cosmos is finite,' 'The cosmos is infinite,' 'The soul and the body are the same,' 'The soul is one thing and the body another,' 'After death a Tathagata exists,' 'After death a Tathagata does not exist,' 'After death a Tathagata both exists and does not exist,' 'After death a Tathagata neither exists nor does not exist' — I don't approve, I don't accept that the Blessed One has not declared them to me. I'll go ask the Blessed One about this matter. If he declares to me that 'The cosmos is eternal,' that 'The cosmos is not eternal,' that 'The cosmos is finite,' that 'The cosmos is infinite,' that 'The soul and the body are the same,' that 'The soul is one thing and the body another,' that 'After death a Tathagata exists,' that 'After death a Tathagata does not exist,' that 'After death a Tathagata both exists and does not exist,' or that 'After death a Tathagata neither exists nor does not exist,' then I will live the holy life under him. If he does not declare to me that 'The cosmos is eternal,'... or that 'After death a Tathagata neither exists nor does not exist,' then I will renounce the training and return to the lower life."[1]

Questions of this sort preoccupied the philosophers of the orthodox Hindu schools to such a degree that they would write lengthy tracts arguing for their own views and refuting, with vigorous logical fisticuffs, the views of all opponents. In a few of his discourses, the Buddha himself engages such questions directly— for example, in the great *Brahmajala Sutta*, where he lays out sixty-two different speculative views. Thus, for a man of his time

---

[1] Thanissaro Bhikkhu (trans.), "The Shorter Instructions to Malunkya," *Majjhima Nikaya* 63. Access to Insight, 1998 http://www.accesstoinsight.org/tipitaka/mn/mn.063.than.html.

and place, to be concerned with metaphysical questions would not have been thought unreasonable; nor would Malunkyaputta have been seen as blameworthy for abandoning a guru who couldn't answer his pressing life-questions. How does the Buddha respond?

"Malunkyaputta, did I ever say to you, 'Come, Malunkyaputta, live the holy life under me, and I will declare to you that 'The cosmos is eternal,' or 'The cosmos is not eternal,' or 'The cosmos is finite,' or 'The cosmos is infinite,' or 'The soul and the body are the same,' or 'The soul is one thing and the body another,' or 'After death a Tathagata exists,' or 'After death a Tathagata does not exist,' or 'After death a Tathagata both exists and does not exist,' or 'After death a Tathagata neither exists nor does not exist'?"

"No, lord."

"And did you ever say to me, 'Lord, I will live the holy life under the Blessed One and [in return] he will declare to me that 'The cosmos is eternal,' or 'The cosmos is not eternal,' or 'The cosmos is finite,' or 'The cosmos is infinite,' or 'The soul and the body are the same,' or 'The soul is one thing and the body another,' or 'After death a Tathagata exists,' or 'After death a Tathagata does not exist,' or 'After death a Tathagata both exists and does not exist,' or 'After death a Tathagata neither exists nor does not exist'?"

"No, lord."

"Then that being the case, foolish man, who are you to be claiming grievances/making demands of anyone?"[2]

Answering questions of this kind was never part of the deal, he says: I never promised to, and you never requested it of me— so why are you suddenly so insistent? Clearly the disciple has

---

[2] Thanissaro, "The Shorter Instructions to Malunkya."

been seized by a philosophical anxiety attack, in which he feels that he can't go on, can't breathe, can't find any sense in things, unless the Buddha delivers conclusive answers that can give meaning and direction to his spiritual life. People commonly go to gurus with questions about eternity, infinity, and immortality, and feel soothed when an answer is given that they can understand. The Buddha's refusal to give Malunkyaputta any answer to these is a deliberate denial of intellectual comfort; this disciple is not allowed the great speculative safety-nets that will rescue him from his fall into meaninglessness. Why not?

"It's just as if a man were wounded with an arrow thickly smeared with poison. His friends and companions, kinsmen and relatives would provide him with a surgeon, and the man would say, 'I won't have this arrow removed until I know whether the man who wounded me was a noble warrior, a brahman, a merchant, or a worker.' He would say, 'I won't have this arrow removed until I know the given name and clan name of the man who wounded me... until I know whether he was tall, medium, or short... until I know whether he was dark, ruddy-brown, or golden-colored... until I know his home village, town, or city... until I know whether the bow with which I was wounded was a long bow or a crossbow... until I know whether the bowstring with which I was wounded was fiber, bamboo threads, sinew, hemp, or bark... until I know whether the shaft with which I was wounded was wild or cultivated... until I know whether the feathers of the shaft with which I was wounded were those of a vulture, a stork, a hawk, a peacock, or another bird... until I know whether the shaft with which I was wounded was bound with the sinew of an ox, a water buffalo, a langur, or a monkey.' He would say, 'I won't have this arrow removed until I know whether the shaft with which I was wounded was that of a common arrow, a curved arrow, a barbed, a calf-toothed, or an oleander arrow.' The man would die and those things would still remain unknown to him."[3]

Like all of us, Malunkyaputta is in trouble: he is unhappy, dissatisfied, not getting what he wants and getting instead what he doesn't want, and secretly in dread of debilitating illness and mortality. His pursuit of grand speculative answers is a distraction from the urgency of his real plight, which involves the removal of the poisoned arrow of his suffering. What he needs to do is to continue practicing mindfulness and to understand the true causes of his discontent, and not waste time with enthralling intellectual puzzles that go nowhere.

Can Malunkyaputta be satisfied with a response like this? The Buddha's advice at first sounds similar to the typical anti-intellectual's exhortation to "do, don't think," and the active man's preference for *real* work as opposed to mere thought or study. Yet such a view rests in a false separation of thought and action; after all, is there any human action that does not depend on a thought concerning how things are and what is worth doing? All our actions stem from some opinion or assumption about ends. Furthermore, do our views about ends not depend on our thoughts about matters like eternity and the nature of the soul? How can a thoughtful human being not think about such matters and not try to seek answers to them? The mind cannot just stop—especially if it thinks it has good reason to keep thinking. A person of noble integrity would never just take someone's word that speculative thinking is a wasteful distraction—because how could you *know*, without actually taking the effort to know, that a clear and definite conclusion could not be reached? Malunkyaputta himself seems more eager to have someone "declare" the truth to him than to struggle for the light himself, and this may be why the Buddha is intentionally thwarting and provoking

---

[3] Thanissaro, "The Shorter Instructions to Malunkya."

him. His next statement deserves careful chewing.

> "Malunkyaputta, it's not the case that when there is the
> view, 'The cosmos is eternal,' there is the living of the holy
> life. And it's not the case that when there is the view, 'The
> cosmos is not eternal,' there is the living of the holy life.
> When there is the view, 'The cosmos is eternal,' and when
> there is the view, 'The cosmos is not eternal,' there is still
> the birth, there is the aging, there is the death, there is the
> sorrow, lamentation, pain, despair, and distress whose de-
> struction I make known right in the here and now."

This looks like the kind of thing a classical Skeptic would say.
For one thing, whenever we convince ourselves of the truth of
one of these positions, our minds still doubt and cannot avoid
considering arguments to the contrary—unless of course we
forcefully suppress the thought that we *could* be wrong, in which
case the act of suppression requires more energy than would have
been spent on the doubting. Whether doubting or suppressing
doubt, the mind is not at peace and therefore cannot offer an
intellectual foundation for a good life. Moreover, would thinking
that the cosmos is eternal or non-eternal have any effect on your
decisions in this life? Does the thought that the soul is the same
as the body make you more or less likely to lead a good life?—
after all, if it dies with the body, you might make this short life
the best and most beautiful possible, or you might become cal-
lous and indifferent to good or bad and simply seek pleasure.
And if the soul is different from the body and does not die with
it, you might become a better person in order to nurture the
long-term good of the soul, or you might not be too concerned
with how you live this tiny life because "deserts of vast eternity"
stretch out before you. More empirically, we also know very good
people who believe the soul to be different from the body, and
very bad people who believe the same thing. A cocaine addict,
even when convinced of what perfect health might look like,

might still sink deeper in his addiction—not because he doesn't have the correct view of health, but because the correct view of health appears abstract and remote from the decisions he is capable of taking at the moment. Therefore the particular lives we lead seem to have very little to do with our speculative views, which have power to fascinate with the lure of distant possibilities but very little power to touch us where we live.

> And why are they undeclared by me? Because they are not connected with the goal, are not fundamental to the holy life. They do not lead to disenchantment, dispassion, cessation, calming, direct knowledge, self-awakening, Unbinding. That's why they are undeclared by me.
>
> And what is declared by me? 'This is dukkha (suffering),' is declared by me. 'This is the origination of dukkha,' is declared by me. 'This is the cessation of dukkha,' is declared by me. 'This is the path of practice leading to the cessation of dukkha,' is declared by me. And why are they declared by me? Because they are connected with the goal, are fundamental to the holy life. They lead to disenchantment, dispassion, cessation, calming, direct knowledge, self-awakening, Unbinding. That's why they are declared by me.[4]

Such views have no practical effect on the state of our soul: whichever speculative view we hold, the decisions that affect our happiness or unhappiness do not depend on them, and it is those decisions that are undertaken on the Buddha's path. It is not an anti-intellectual path, because the decisions that genuinely affect us require scrupulous thought and a good deal of insight into the workings of heart and mind—but it is also not a path that has much patience for abstract theorizing and speculative "play." In

---

[4] Thanissaro, "The Shorter Instructions to Malunkya."

many cultures the opposition to speculative thinking springs from materialistic assumptions that only physical things are real and that financial realities are physical, but the Buddha is not a materialist. All practical activity comes from ways of thinking and prior states of the soul, and these have to be perceived, understood, and addressed if we wish to free ourselves from agitation and distress. This is not anti-intellectual, but it is pragmatic in a way that embraces a comprehension of intellectual activity.

In other discourses, the Buddha or one of his close disciples will amplify on why it is that many thinkers cling to broad speculative views and why they are wrong to do so—for example, when the monk Moggallana replies to the Brahmin ascetic Vacchagotta with the exact words the Buddha has used elsewhere:

> "Now, Master Moggallana, what is the cause, what is the reason why — when wanderers of other sects are asked in this way, they answer that 'The cosmos is eternal' or 'The cosmos is not eternal' or 'The cosmos is finite' or 'The cosmos is infinite' or 'The body is the same as the soul' or 'The body is one thing and the soul another' or 'The Tathagata exists after death' or 'The Tathagata does not exist after death' or 'The Tathagata both exists and does not exist after death" or 'The Tathagata neither exists nor does not exist after death,' yet when Gotama the contemplative is asked in this way, he does not answer that 'The cosmos is eternal' or 'The cosmos is not eternal' or 'The cosmos is finite' or 'The cosmos is infinite' or 'The body is the same as the soul' or 'The body is one thing and the soul another' or 'The Tathagata exists after death' or 'The Tathagata does not exist after death' or 'The Tathagata both exists and does not exist after death" or 'The Tathagata neither exists nor does not exist after death'?"
>
> "Vaccha, the members of other sects assume of the eye that 'This is mine, this is my self, this is what I am.' They

assume of the ear... the nose... the tongue... the body... the intellect that 'This is mine, this is my self, this is what I am.' That is why, when asked in this way, they answer that 'The cosmos is eternal'... or that 'The Tathagata neither exists nor does not exist after death.' But the Tathagata, worthy and rightly self-awakened, does not assume of the eye that 'This is mine, this is my self, this is what I am.' He does not assume of the ear... the nose... the tongue... the body... the intellect that 'This is mine, this is my self, this is what I am.' That is why, when asked in this way, he does not answer that 'The cosmos is eternal'... or that 'The Tathagata neither exists nor does not exist after death.'" [5]

In other words, these thinkers crave certainty with regard to speculative views because each one of them has in some way identified themselves with their aggregates, the fundamental constituents of what they take to be "who they are," and are so powerfully invested in their identification that they unconsciously project it onto the larger-than-life screen of speculation. Thus the "solving of great questions" is often a form of spiritual ambition, which originates in habit and compulsion. If we could see into the activity through which a self and its projections are continuously made, our passion for far-flung speculation would naturally dissipate, like steam.

[5] Thanissaro Bhikkhu (trans.) "Moggallana Sutta," *Samyutta Nikaya* 44:7, Access to Insight, 2004. http://www.accesstoinsight.org/tipitaka/sn/sn44/sn44.007.than.html.

16. Eating Ice Cream with the Buddha

The words of the Buddha, as they are given to us in the Pali Canon, can seem abstract, highly theoretical, dry. But dry-as-dust they are not, for there are so many other ways of being dry. High mountain air is gloriously, bracingly dry. Kindling for fire-wood is dry, and the drier it is, the fiercer the initial blaze. A ship's cabin is a delightful haven of dryness when a sea storm rages all around; and when we come in from the storm, dry ourselves off, and put on dry clothes, we feel human again. The impression of dryness comes from the Buddha's analytical rigor: in all of his teachings he analyzes and interrogates our experience, but the analysis is powerful only because his observation of experience is accurate, keen, respectful. Indeed, he challenges us to confront our own experience truthfully and bravely—and not just believe our feelings, because we all tend to go along with our fears and desires without asking what they really are. First we observe, and then we question. In doing this we will really risk something of ourselves, in return for something that we might not want right now: sanity, clarity, understanding.

This essay is the first of four in which I will ponder one small section of a single sutta as fully as I can, with a view to understanding something momentous: how exactly discontent and unhappiness arise.

At the heart of the Buddha's teaching is the Chain of Dependent Origination, which turns up throughout the texts in slightly different versions, with small variations, but substantially the same. In this chain the Buddha presents in shorthand form the origin of suffering through a series of conditions, starting with embodied existence. Everything in the Buddha's teaching can be found in this chain, and at the beginning of its most powerful presentation, the *Mahanidana Sutta* ("Greater Discourse on Causation"), the stalwart disciple Ananda is told to beware of thinking that he has understood it, since it is a bottomless and subtle doctrine. In this essay I want to focus on the connection between feeling, craving, and clinging; indeed, the Buddha himself dwells on craving in this particular Sutta, as if of all the links it is the one we can see most clearly.

Here is the whole chain of dependent origination, from the *Mahanidana*:

> "Thus, Ananda, with mentality-materality as condition there is consciousness; with consciousness as condition there is materiality-mentality; with mentality-materiality as condition there is contact; with contact as condition there is feeling; with feeling as condition there is craving; with craving as condition there is clinging; with clinging as condition there is existence; with existence as condition there is birth; and with birth as condition, aging and death, sorrow, lamentation, pain, grief, and despair come to be. Such is the origin of this entire mass of suffering." [1]

On first reading, the chain comes across as so compact that it is impenetrable. The obscure phrase "materiality-mentality" translates *nama-rupa*, literally "name and form," which is shorthand for the psycho-physical complex that grounds all organic life. Organic life always comes with some form of *consciousness*, which includes primitive sentience but also the apparent teleological sense that we see in organisms: the cell "knows" how to grow and function, and how to relate with the cells around it; the plant "knows" the movement of the sun, the changing of the sea-

---

[1] Bhikkhu Bodhi (trans.), *Mahanidana Sutta, Digha Nikaya* 15, SuttaCentral, 1984. https://suttacentral.net/en/dn15.

sons, how to nurse itself back to health if it is injured. All organic life has *nama-rupa* and *consciousness*, reciprocally dependent: take one away and the other goes. But it also has varied and manifold capacities for sensation, which requires *contact* of our sense organs (including the mind, the interior sense) with their objects. Every sensation is accompanied by some kind of *feeling*. Crudely, feeling, or *vedana*, may be boiled down to pleasure, pain, and neutral, but there are infinite gradations of these, and infinite combinations of feelings not easy to categorize. The key is that we are embodied, conscious beings with various capacities for sensing and perceiving, and when we experience, something happens at the sensory level that is more than merely sensing. For instance, when our taste buds encounter a new kind of ice cream we may experience sweetness and other taste sensations, but there is nearly always a feeling of something like pleasure or pain. And then what happens?

To answer this, we need to be aware of what we experience. Seeing what the Buddha is seeing always demands not just thinking but also the practice of focused awareness, which he has described in the *Satipatthana Sutta*: we have to attend to our experience, notice what happens, and see how it changes from moment to moment. When we are novices to this practice, the observations will be more crudely delineated, but with time and effort we become more sensitive and start to notice more. The Suttas speak to us when we root them in actual experience.

This is what happens. A friend gives us a scoop of a new brand of ice cream. We taste it. It is sweet, unique, vanilla and chocolate and some nut. Mmmmm. We like it. What's it called? Can I have seconds? Next time we go to the store we will get some. In fact, it is so good that we need to keep some in the freezer all the time...All this usually takes place in a moment, apparently as a single, unified reaction to the first taste. Occasionally the last part—the decision to keep some on hand always—might be delayed, but most of the time there is no transition between the first taste and the polishing off of the entire portion. If we focus carefully on this experience, there are three distinct phases, of which only the first may be unavoidable: 1) the actual sensation of taste: sweet, yum; 2) the desire for more; 3) the determination to secure it for the future. In Buddhist jargon, 1) is feeling, 2) is craving (*tanha*, literally "thirst"), 3) is clinging or attachment. The taste itself is innocuous; there is nothing unwholesome or hazardous about liking a sensation. But what happens after this? Is the move from feeling to craving inevitable?

We can always stop after the first spoonful of ice cream, the first square of chocolate, the first sip of wine—just as we can stop after the first bowl, the first bar, the first glass. Why do we usually not stop? We are trying to repeat the pleasurable experience of the first spoon, as if we really thought that it could be repeated. After all, we know rationally that we cannot experience the same thing twice in exactly the same way; life just doesn't work that way. So we finish the bowl and even ask for a second helping; in fact, usually as we eat, the next spoon is loaded while the current blob of ice cream is still in our mouths, as we attempt to experience an uninterrupted flow of the same pleasure.

In contrast, someone who is trying to recover from sugar addiction is well aware of the heightened pleasure of allowing himself only one spoonful; the taste is better if we are not expecting to repeat it, and we relish it more intensely. A friend of mine once weaned himself from the need to have five mugs of coffee every morning, and after a week of hard austerity he realized that one mug of coffee tasted much better and that he no longer felt he needed the other four. The desire to repeat is a compulsion, and when it is cured, we enjoy the present more. In fact, the compulsion—when it is experienced as an unavoidable necessity—leads to less pleasure, a kind of dullness, which, when it is how we experience everything we eat and drink, spreads like a grime of discontent over our everyday lives.

We drink one beer: why do we think we need another? We eat one scoop of ice cream: why do we think we have to have two? It takes a psychological genius like the Buddha to see clearly that we are, miraculously, *capable* of asking this question—which means that the step from one scoop of ice cream to two is not inevitable, not a natural necessity. If we think it is inevitable, we will suffer—because we will feel thwarted and dissatisfied if we cannot get it (and we can't, because it simply won't taste the same twice!). If we see that it is not inevitable, we start to free ourselves from imagined needs—and once we realize that this is possible, and that we might become happier because of it, we can practice it, first by paying attention, and then by interrogating the compulsion. We do not need to obey our desires blindly and helplessly.

Amazingly, once we break the fetter of compulsion between one beer and two, we find ourselves free of the compulsion for even one beer. If it is offered, great; if not, water tastes pretty good too—and when we realize that water is not in itself less of a sensation than beer, but indeed can be just as interesting and pleasurable, we will find ourselves journeying on a path towards more autonomy and contentment. Our joys will be more joyful if we don't expect to repeat them; we will notice and feel with greater clarity, and to the extent that every moment is new, we will finally be able to experience the new and not just the repeated. Is it not sad, when we eat a bowl of ice cream, to discover that we only really tasted the first spoonful and that all the others were only attempted repetitions of the memory? The first taste was an experience; the subsequent ones were lost experiences.

So far the examples I have chosen to understand the transition from feeling to craving have had to do with sensory pleasures. It is easy to see that our reaction to sensory pain or displeasure is just as much a form of craving, but a craving to flee. We taste something "bad," and instantly move to wanting never again to meet this taste or anything resembling it. Craving includes both attraction and aversion. If we generalize the taste example to experiences through all the other senses—visual beauty, auditory pleasure, olfactory and tactile titillation—we can easily see how, if we think through this in all of our sensory experience and notice clearly that there is no necessary bond between feeling and craving, our lives would be transformed and much more interesting.

17. Perpetual Ice Cream

The ice cream meets our tongue, we utter the sacred syllable *mmmmmmm*, and find ourselves automatically slurping the whole scoop and sometimes a second or a third one: this is the move from "feeling" to "craving," and while it may be a "natural" move, it is not an inevitable one. This is why the Buddha always speaks of "condition," not "cause"; it is a subtle and important distinction. "With feeling as *condition* there is craving; with craving as condition there is clinging; with clinging as condition there is existence." If feeling *caused* craving, whenever our senses met a sense object, craving would spring unavoidably from the sensation. But we have seen in our own experience that that is not so: we can be satisfied with one taste of ice cream, with one cup of tea. Therefore feeling is only a *condition* for craving: if there were no feeling, there would be no craving. A person deaf from birth would not crave Bach; a dog probably craves many more olfactory objects than we do, since dogs can smell whole universes of things that we cannot even notice. The Buddha is not telling us to stop feeling just because it is a condition of craving; we can't, as long as our senses bump into the things they are meant to sense. We can, however, weaken or sever the link between feeling and craving, once we become aware of this link and know that it is not inevitable. It is not that we *should* not be subject to craving, but that when we glimpse that craving does not lead to happiness we will naturally slow down and look more carefully whenever we experience feeling turning to craving.

One of the beauties of this is that the kind of attention that is asked of us can be practiced—not only understood, but embodied in our acts of attention: anywhere, at any time, by anybody. Understanding and practice are foundations for each other. Before going on to feeling and craving in our relation to non-sensory objects, let's dwell a little on the next two links in the chain: how craving conditions clinging (or attachment), and how clinging conditions "existence." This will give us a deeper understanding of the significance of craving.

After polishing off all the ice cream in front of us, and if we decide that we like it, we usually have something resembling this thought: I've got to buy some and keep it in my freezer—or, This is so good I must never again be without it. A milder version is: I won't get some now but I know where I can get some if I suddenly decide I want it. These three variations are basically the same thought, because they all involve the perceived need to secure a future supply of the now cherished object. Thus, when we pay money for the ice cream, what we are buying is not only the present container but the certainty of future ice cream: the industrially farmed cows to make enough ice cream for millions of people with this craving, the people employed in the handling of cows and the production of ice cream, all the machines and the people who build them and the mining that provides materials for them, the freezer-trucks to guarantee a supply through all four seasons of the year, the truck-drivers, a stable and dependable source of oil for the trucks, the maintenance of that dependability through military action, and so on. This is true of attachment to any sense object—food, drink, clothes, and most other things we buy.

Attachment or clinging is the attempt to secure the endless satisfaction of our cravings, most commonly by funding the materials, construction, and labor in and around the objects of our desires: perpetual ice cream by definition presupposes perpetuity of all the other things that go into ice cream. If you perform an analytical meditation on one or two things you know you cling to—chocolate, coffee, liquor—you will see in a very short time that while these things present a simple surface to us, what the surface masks is almost an entire world of activity that we unconsciously participate in building in order to satisfy craving. Moreover, we generally want to satisfy cravings as cheaply as possible, so that we have more money left over to satisfy other cravings; and this means we are perfectly okay with getting more from the world than we can pay for.

The same applies to the craving for biological life, in which clinging manifests in such phenomena as having children and health insurance, not to mention military defense—all of which are supported by billions of hours of labor and other sacrifices. The word translated as "clinging" or "attachment," *upadana*, literally means *fuel*: fuel for craving, fuel for the world created by craving. This is what the Buddha means by "clinging conditions existence": it makes the world, and the world is thus an expression of the collective cravings of all the beings in it. Characteristically, the Buddha does not instruct us to judge this state of things, but only to observe and understand it: when we look it fully in the face, do we like it, does it disturb us, can we be content with it? If it is possible for us to go through life never confronting craving and clinging, it will be because we secretly know that if we thought about it we would not be at peace.

When we apply the same analytical insight to non-sensory objects such as career, relationships, beliefs, and ideas about things like selves or souls, we might find ourselves even more deeply unsettled.

18. Clinging for Dear Life
(1) Vocation

Could my life's work also be a result of craving and clinging? Let's revisit that first taste of ice cream. When we try, we find that we can observe our moment-by-moment experience of sensory pleasures to catch those exact points at which a feeling of liking turns into a compulsion to have more, and the compulsion to have more turns into the necessity of securing the permanent availability of that pleasure: this process is the turn from feeling to craving to clinging, which can happen in an instant and feel completely natural and unavoidable. But when we pay attention to our experience, we discover that we can put our spoon down whenever we want, and that if we never experience this pleasure again that will be just dandy. Clinging or attachment (I use these words interchangeably to translate *upadana*) is basically the desire to repeat, even though we know that we can never repeat anything anyway, because nothing stays the same. It is clinging that then creates the systems and structures to guarantee the repetition: the money we pay for our tub of ice cream is not just so that we may have it in our fridge, but so that it continues to be made and transported, and our favorite grocery store continues to stock it. Our clinging to sense pleasures—edibles, potables, and wearables make up just a small part of them—commits us to maintaining a vast supply line of labor and production, which then holds us in cycles of securing and security that soon feel like prisons. Our attachment to the myriad benefits of petroleum, for instance, while it may begin as a liking for the personal freedom that comes with cars, creates a world that is full of trouble and unsustainable entanglements. There is nothing wrong with liking that first spoon of ice cream, and indeed nothing wrong with what follows—just that if we move automatically from liking to clinging, we will lose the sharpness and definition of the first encounter in the increasing dullness of something like an addiction. And the attempt to secure an attachment will usually lead to conflict (as the Buddha explains in a later passage in the *Mahanidana Sutta*).[1]

Craving and clinging occur not only in attraction to sense objects, but also in aversion to them. A chronic avoidance of exercise, for example, might express a craving for comfort that becomes a clinging. Fear of the pain of toothaches leads to a craving to avoid them, which then creates dental insurance and the hours of work needed to pay for that. Indeed, fear of pain, in illness or dying, generates an abundance of avoidance strategies.

Our experience of sense objects can be watched, slowed down, and analyzed with some acumen. Sometimes thinking through the consequences of clinging can be enough to make us not want to have the experience again—for instance, when we know the health effects of certain foods. But what about objects of experience that are not sensory? The Buddha says there is such a thing as craving for mental objects (*Mahanidana Sutta*, 7) and in addition to clinging to sense pleasures, he mentions clinging to views, clinging to precepts and observances, clinging to a doctrine of self (*Mahanidana*, 6). These are much more difficult to notice, and just noticing them may require more disciplined training. We will go more into views and doctrines of the self in another essay, but here I would like to offer a couple of examples of craving for mental objects as the tiny first shoots of what might become a mighty, many-branched tree of investigation. Mental objects pass from feeling to craving to clinging in much the same way as a taste of ice cream does.

---

[1] Bhikkhu Bodhi, *Mahanidana Sutta, Digha Nikaya* 15.

Here is a teenager who reads a lot. She begins the first volume of a new fantasy series, loves it, is immediately "hooked." She has to finish the whole book. Then she has to finish the whole series. Probably she will buy it in order to have it available for re-reading, or just to know that she has it. Her buying it is the beginning of a collection, because after this first series she will have to read more complete fantasy series; and after this, all works by the same authors. When she has read this, whenever she goes to the Amazon website or into a large bookshop, she will feel quite tangibly a craving for similar writings. Of course, the craving cannot be satisfied, because no subsequent book will be the same as the first read, and if she seeks to replicate her formative experience she is going to feel something like a twinge of empty futility. Often at this point the craving, having run out of things of the same kind to read, has to change its focus if there is to be even the semblance of satisfaction, and our young reader starts reading grown-up authors, but with the same hungry compulsiveness. The attachment is already deep—because if she were deprived of anything to read, she would be unhappy, and might even feel a terrible desperation.

However, the next stage of attachment is more interesting: the need to secure the enjoyment of reading. Because of her highly developed skills as a reader, by now she shines in certain subjects at school and has been given some encouragement. "I am going to study literature in college," she decides—and from there it is a short step to "I am going to be a writer" or "I am going to be a scholar." The attachment has been transformed into a sense of vocation, which may linger in this person for decades, even though they may spend those decades working in an office or a restaurant. I am not saying this is how it works for everyone; it was like this for me, and for many people I know. The attachment can be complex, a compounding of different people's attachments: for example, when a father's deep clinging to a security and success that he himself never attained gets projected onto the son, who takes it as his own.

In fact usually our sense of vocation or inner attraction to a career is composite, made up of other people's clingings of which we are barely aware. It never simply *is*. But as we grow older in our various occupations, and indeed become soft-wired by them to think and act in certain ways, it becomes harder to look at our relationship with them objectively. We become identified with them, and find it difficult to detach ourselves from the identification. It can become harder and harder even to imagine a practical alternative for ourselves.

The same difficulty exists in cases where we identify with vocations that we have not pursued and that have lingered in the background of our lives. I once met a woman at a party who seemed miserable and close to tears. I asked her what was wrong, and she told me she had that day had a vivid realization: she had for forty years considered herself an artist, and thought that that was what she was meant to be but she had done no art for all that time—and so she could not possibly be an artist, could she? What she saw clearly was that the artistic identity had formed early and was honest and powerful at the time, but since then she had changed and was no longer that person—while all the time thinking of herself as that person, lugging that person around with her wherever she went. For some reason that she had yet to figure out, it had been essential for her to think of herself as an artist. To perceive now that she was in truth not an artist but a fantasized artist was a shattering blow to her, because something fundamental to her self-image had been eradicated. She did not know who she was any more. She had witnessed her own clinging to a possibly fabricated self-image, and her current misery came from witnessing the degree of this attachment; she felt broken. Was it a good thing to have had this realization? Most people at this point will replace the broken self-image with a new illusion, but this woman bravely preferred to sit with it.

Everything changes; we change. One day we walk out of our houses and see that there are buds on the trees: "Oh, spring's here. My, it came suddenly." But in fact nothing happened suddenly, it all happened moment by moment at its usual pace, and we failed to notice it: we were still living in winter while winter was in process of turning to spring. Just so, with ourselves: we do not notice ourselves changing, we assume that we stay still while everything else changes, and all of a sudden—often through some crisis—we discover that we have lost ourselves. We had been living encased in attachment to a static self-image that became harder and harder to shed because the rest of our lives organized itself around preserving it.

Thus in hurtling onto a life path we find feeling turning to craving turning to clinging. The initial love of a book did not *have* to lead to reading the whole series. I could have stopped there, and then decided to read something different, or not read at all. Continuing to read also did not *have* to lead to a life built around reading, although at the time the alternatives seemed inconceivable. I could have enjoyed reading, and then decided to build my life on something else. None of the transitions was necessary—but it all *felt* necessary: "I *have* to do this." Seeing this clearly for what it is, namely the apparently natural move from feeling to craving to clinging, we might still choose the same things we chose, but we wouldn't feel compelled. Indeed, the absence of compulsion is nothing other than freedom.

Do the same insights apply to that other great hurtling—our love life, the hurtling of our hearts?

19. Clinging for Dear Life
(2) Love

The most exciting thing about the Buddhist practice of mindfulness is the discovery that there is no such thing as a small or insignificant experience. If you are attentive to what goes on when you do something as simple as taste, you will find yourself holding the key to all other experiences.

Feeling, then craving, then clinging: we've seen when observing ourselves taste ice cream that feeling is unavoidable as long as we have the sense organ to sense with and the sense object to sense, but that clinging and craving—the desire for more, and the compulsion to secure the pleasant feeling—present themselves as an immediate component of feeling while they are in fact not intrinsic to it. We cannot help liking the sweetness of good chocolate ice cream, but when we gobble up the whole bowl and rush to the store to buy more we are acting automatically and unthinkingly, assuming that this is a natural chain of events that necessarily spills out of the first taste—and we are frustrated, disappointed, sometimes angry, when the chain is interrupted. But we know we can easily train ourselves not to need more than the first taste, and therefore we know that craving and clinging are in fact not intrinsic to feeling: we can feel, notice, enjoy, and move on. We do not have to be locked into the initial feeling, in the hope of repeating it. We've seen how in the case of pleasures our clinging leads to the creation of a world that is built upon the guaranteed satisfaction of our pleasures; and in the case of our displeasure, our clinging structures our world such that unpleasantness can be avoided. The pleasure can be relatively simple: good food, good drink, nice clothes, nice car, cheap gas, cheap utilities. The displeasures can also be simple: pain, illness, death. We spend most of our physical and mental energy working to secure the pleasures and ward off the displeasures. There are more subtle versions of these too: music, the arts, the cultivated pleasures; and there are also ideas we dislike, things we would rather not think about, regarding which we work hard to secure our ignorance—for example, what happens with our waste, who grows our food, how exactly our peace and safety are maintained. The clinging pervades and orders our lives, and as long as we are unconscious of it we cannot really be free.

The unthinking drift from feeling to clinging is easy to notice in a sense experience such as taste, partly because in such experiences nothing big is at stake and we have nothing we feel we need to hide from ourselves. But what if we encounter people in much the same way as we encounter taste pleasures? It is difficult to achieve awareness of how we relate to other people because so much of our way of relating is bound up with who we think we are or who we fear we might be. We would in fact rather not look at ourselves too closely. When we meet someone we find delightful, and enjoy the first encounter because of similarity of interests, attractive appearance, the pleasure of finding someone else interested in us, and a compatible tempo in speech and thought, it is easy to slip into a belief that there was a deep pre-existing bond, something significant underlying the meeting that gives it its "destined" feel. We go home wondering if this person is "the one," and for days after might even fantasize about future encounters or a future life with this new person. This move from feeling—that first delight—to craving and then clinging, in which we actively take steps to secure the delight, feels perfectly natural, and is much more intense and pervasive than any mere sense pleasure. We easily become obsessed, because we feel that our happiness is invested. The initial attraction may lead quickly to the desire for sexual intimacy; our entire gender identities are suddenly at stake, our "manhood" or "womanhood," and being rebuffed can hurt us deeply. Yet most often, when acted upon, the desire for intimacy is disillusioning, and pursuit can bring on complications that have more pain than pleasure. When that happens, we may realize that in the first marvelous encounter we were already getting everything we could want from this person: the encounter was perfect, there was nothing lacking. The need to have more was not at all intrinsic to the situation, and whenever we insist that we must have more we are in fact pushing the encounter beyond the bounds of delight into more troubled territory. We see this in clinging that is not only sexual but romantic.

The Buddha points out that one of the non-sensory objects of clinging is our idea of self—for example, that we have a permanent self underneath the changing being we actually experience from day to day, that this self has a nature and something like a destiny, that its reality is confirmed by other selves with whom it is meant to be, with whom it has a profound and meaningful bond. Romantic clinging is one of the most powerful expressions of clinging to an idea of self, and it is so powerful that a romantic person clings to the clinging itself, becoming angry when it is questioned. The idea that the person we just met and to whom we are irresistibly attracted has a deep unbreakable bond with us is a form of clinging because in our minds we have already managed to render permanent the delight of the first encounter; there, in our minds, it is much more than a meeting in the moment. When we act on the attachment, and seek not only more dates but something like marriage, the mental clinging is given legal and physical form.

Just as we attempt to make a wonderful ice-cream constantly available to us because we like the first taste so much, here we want to make sure that the good romantic feeling of the first encounters never goes away: the golden days become the ideal for the whole relationship, and we strive to relive them whenever we can and are always reminding ourselves of them. This is what Valentine's Day and anniversaries are for: ritualized repetition. Couples who have been married for a few years and suddenly notice that the old romantic feeling is no longer there—neither in their partner nor themselves—can find themselves in despair or panic, as if the whole relationship has now lost its meaning. They never really thought about what it meant to know that everything changes, that nothing stays the same, especially thoughts and feelings. Since all attachments are essentially a desire for repetition, a hope that something will stay the same, therefore all attachments are doomed to disappointment, because nothing *can* be repeated. If our relationship is founded on a hope of repeating the golden days forever, even if only internally, by holding them up as a standard to measure all subsequent days, we will surely be miserable and unfulfilled—because in everything, "then is then and now is now."

Does that mean that a commitment like marriage is sheer folly, because no one can possibly know they will stay constant? Perhaps. If it is not to be folly, it will have to be built on something other than a desire to repeat or maintain; it must be built rather on a knowledge that every moment is new, and that the partners will be new each day, and that the commitment is to navigate together through the new and unexpected—which will include physical and mental illness, long cycles of anger and frustration, and the derangements of suffering. Marriage then becomes a frightening adventure—undertaken with that magical someone who has a true love of adventure with all its dangers, who understands that the golden days of romance were only a beginning to be moved beyond, and that what follows will bring hardships and joys that will always be surprising. Perhaps only very few people can do that, but those who can will surely have welcoming good humor and generosity towards their troublesome, unpredictable partners and—more difficultly—towards themselves.

20. How Can We Eat for Pleasure?
"The Parable of the Son's Flesh."

Hidden away in the vast collection of the Buddha's teachings called the *Connected Discourses* (*Samyutta Nikaya*) we discover what is perhaps the bleakest and most powerful of his parables, "The Son's Flesh"[1] (12.63; I quote the main part in full at the end of this essay). It is one of those teachings that can act like a bucket of icy water on a drunk man. In it, a family of three—mother, father, son—are crossing a desert. They have run out of food and water, yet still have a stretch of desert to cross before reaching an oasis. Are they all going to die, or is there only hope that two of them might make it if they eat the third? If so, who will be killed and eaten? After some deliberation, they decide to eat the child, possibly because it is already in a more weakened state than the others; or because the family unit is stronger if both parents survive. They kill him, and by rationing out the dried and roasted meat over the ensuing week they manage to reach the oasis. The crucial part of the parable is not the killing and eating, but the parents' feelings about it. Will they *enjoy* the taste of the meat, or take an iota of pleasure in it? *No*, the Buddha's disciples instantly reply, *with each mouthful they will beat their breasts and weep for their child, crying "Child, where are you? Where are you?"* The only reason they are eating it is to get across the desert.

The lesson is about more than the horrors of cannibalism or

---

[1] Nyanaponika Thera (trans.), "The Discourse on 'Son's Flesh', or The Similes for the Four Nutriments," in *The Four Nutriments of Life*. Access to Insight, 2006. www.accesstoinsight.org/lib/authors/nyanaponika/wheel105.html.

of carnivorous life. It is given in the context of a series of teachings about the "nutrients," which include biological nutrition, but also sense-impressions, "volitional thought," and consciousness. The "nutrients" are all those things we have to take in, consume, digest, in order to continue existing; they are a sweeping, roaring flood that feeds the life of our being. In this essay I'm going to focus on bodily food, but as we shall see, this notion encompasses not only what we put in our mouths but everything that gives material *and* immaterial support to our continued existence and yet is largely invisible to us.

The food we hold at the end of our fork is not just a lump of edible matter but the whole world of activity that went into its production. There was a cook. There were farmers, usually migrant workers working in inhuman conditions, who do the backbreaking labor of preparing the soil, planting, daily tending, harvesting, gathering, carrying, sorting, and more; often these are children. There are the animals, human beings, native plant species that were driven or burnt off the land so that it could be made to feed a whole population—and the land itself, deteriorating under the pressure. There are the food-plant workers who package the food, the transportation workers who get it to our shop, the retail workers who arrange, store, and sell it to us. The list of sentient beings involved is dizzying to contemplate, and if we are honest we can also admit that we pay as little as possible for this food, shopping where we get the best deal. Because of this it is very difficult for all those people responsible for our food to rise above their often brutal and dehumanizing working lives—lives that we ourselves would never choose to have. We are not to blame for this; we need to be economical in our expenditures, not just for ourselves but for the sakes of those who depend on us. In this process there are also all those machines, tools, vehicles, which are manufactured and have equally complicated conditions of production: they too contain worlds. And all the people involved—including the ones who don't physically labor but who deal with organization and money, and who make the prices "competitive" so that we can afford it, and all those people who invest in food-producing companies so that they stay financially strong—all of these people need to be fed, clothed, sheltered, in other webs of activity: worlds behind worlds behind worlds. And there is the fuel for running and making those machines, for processing the raw agricultural produce, for treating and delivering the fabric for the workers' clothes...and the people and machines, the wars and political coercion, the defense and security apparatus, for guaranteeing that fuel. If we went out and looked, we would see tremendous suffering in these worlds of production, but an intelligent and imaginative person is capable of inferring from such things as low prices, and where this food comes from, that the production of food is not pretty. This is especially true of meat production, of course—which is one reason why slaughter-houses do not have big glass windows. And this is also why the ads and posters for our foodstuffs always show clichéd agrarian idylls and never the actual conditions of food production—because if they did, most people wouldn't want to eat.

All this is sitting in our spoon. It is not mere matter, mere chemical constituents, that we are putting in our mouths—but worlds of activity by millions, actually billions, of beings. When we contemplate this, how is it possible for a thoughtful being to "enjoy" the mouthful? I love my dogs and cats, yet a pig or cow is at least as sensitive and intelligent as my dog Jake, who picks me up when I am down—and if I were to kill and eat Jake simply because I *liked* the taste, would that not be an act of dehumanizing barbarism?—dehumanizing of me, that is. Even more so if I were to repress what I know or infer of the production chain on the other side of my spoon, and mindlessly "enjoy" it as if none of that suffering exists. This is what the Buddha is saying with the Parable of the Son's Flesh. It is not that we *shouldn't* enjoy our food; it is that if we consider it and are aware of what it actually is, how can we? This is not squeamishness, or a puritanical pushing away of pleasure, but the honest response of a humane intelligence that faces squarely the conditions of our existence and does not blink. If you can do that and still enjoy your food, go for it. If you can't enjoy your food any more, at least not as much, you will still eat—but you may be more careful, more respectful, less wasteful, less cavalier: less intoxicated by consumption.

Of course, the Parable of the Son's Flesh concerns much more than food. The sources of energy that fuel our civilization would be another kind of "nutrient." In his 1937 book *The Road to Wigan Pier*, George Orwell vividly described the realities of coal production: how miners would work at a coal face three to four feet high, digging on their knees, each man expecting to produce at a rate of two tons an hour, for over seven hours; how the coal faces could lie as far as five miles from the elevator, to be reached by an arduous trek down low tunnels, a trek comparable in exertion to climbing a small mountain to get to work, and for which the men were not paid; the deafening noise of the machines, the clouds of coal dust, the acrid smell—and above all, how ignorant the above-ground civilization was of this vast subterranean industry that maintained every aspect of its being. The very desk I am writing on may well be perched high above a labyrinth of tunnels down which thousands of human beings less fortunate than I have trudged and sweated, and yet I have been wholly unaware of this.

"You could quite easily drive a car right across the north of England and never once remember that hundreds of feet below the road you are on the miners are hacking at the coal. Yet in a sense it is the miners who are driving your car forward. Their lamp-lit world down there is as necessary to the daylight world above as the root is to the flower," Orwell remarks. "But on the whole we are not aware of it; we all know that we 'must have coal', but we seldom or never remember what coal-getting involves."[2] *Mutatis mutandis*, everything he says can apply to our relation to our primary sources of fuel today. We have an interest in keeping its production invisible, or pretending that it is invisible, because only thus can we consider ourselves "above it" and devoted to higher things. The Parable of the Son's Flesh is a stern reminder of the realities of our consumption, but regular reflection on this austere teaching can detach us at least a little from "healthy callousness" and reconnect us with our fundamental humanity and dignity.

> It is not long since conditions in the mines were worse than they are now. There are still living a few very old women who in their youth have worked underground, with the harness round their waists, and a chain that passed between their legs, crawling on all fours and dragging tubs of coal. They used to go on doing this even when they were pregnant. And even now, if coal could not be produced without pregnant women dragging it to and fro, I fancy we should let them do it rather than deprive ourselves of coal. But most of the time, of course, we should prefer to forget that they were doing it. It is so with all types of manual work; it keeps us alive, and we are oblivious of its existence. More than anyone else, perhaps, the miner can stand as the type of the manual worker, not only because his work is so exaggeratedly awful, but also because it is so vitally necessary and yet so remote from our experience, so invisible, as it were, that we are capable of forgetting it as we forget the blood in our veins. In a way it is even humiliating to watch coal-miners working. It raises in you a momentary doubt

[2] George Orwell, *The Road to Wigan Pier* (London, 1937) chapter 2. www.george-orwell.org/The_Road_to_Wigan_Pier.

about your own status as an 'intellectual' and a superior person generally. For it is brought home to you, at least while you are watching, that it is only because miners sweat their guts out that superior persons can remain superior.[3]

The Son's Flesh (excerpt, *SN* 12.63)

"There are, O monks, four nutriments for the sustenance of beings born, and for the support of beings seeking birth. What are the four?

"Edible food, coarse and fine; secondly, sense-impression; thirdly, volitional thought; fourthly, consciousness.

"How, O monks, should the nutriment edible food be considered? Suppose a couple, husband and wife, have set out on a journey through the desert, carrying only limited provisions. They have with them their only son, dearly beloved by them. Now, while these two traveled through the desert, their limited stock of provisions ran out and came to an end, but there was still a stretch of desert not yet crossed. Then the two thought: 'Our small stock of provisions has run out, it has come to an end; and there is still a stretch of desert that is not yet crossed. Should we not kill our only son, so dearly beloved, prepare dried and roasted meat, and eating our son's flesh, we may cross in that way the remaining part of the desert, lest all three of us perish?'

"And these two, husband and wife, killed their only son, so dearly beloved by them, prepared dried and roasted meat, and, eating their son's flesh, crossed in that way the remaining part of the desert. And while eating their son's flesh, they were beating their breast and crying: 'Where are you, our only and beloved son? Where are you, our only and beloved son?'

"What do you think, O monks? Will they eat the food

---

[3] Orwell, *The Road to Wigan Pier.*

for the pleasure of it, for enjoyment, for comeliness' sake, for (the body's) embellishment?"

"Certainly not, O Lord."

"Will they not rather eat the food merely for the sake of crossing the desert?"

"So it is, O Lord."[4]

---

[4] Nyanaponika Thera, "The Discourse on 'Son's Flesh,' or The Similes for the Four Nutriments."

21. The Buddha's Most Useful Parable

A practitioner of martial arts or any arduous physical activity learns very early on to make clear determinations about *vedana*, or "feelings." You frequently get thumped in the chest or slammed to the ground. If you're a novice, your reaction to this will be panic, dismay, demoralization: rapid heartbeat, heavy breathing, need to surrender. After this has happened a number of times, the reaction is: *I got struck but did it hurt? No—it was only impact but not pain. I can go on.* Later, you get hit in the face, or ski into a tree, or fall from ten feet while climbing, or get thrown to the mat and pinned by a large hairy man. A beginner might fall to pieces in reaction to any of these, but a veteran would pause and investigate calmly: *This hurts, but is it actually injury or only pain and shock? If it is not injury, I can go on...* The difference between a novice and a veteran is that the former doesn't know the possible meanings of impact or pain, so every mishap seems dangerous—while the veteran can distinguish serenely between harmless and injurious, and *respond* rather than *react*. Without awareness and intelligence, one can only react. Such simple (but not easy!) discrimination can be taken to more interesting levels. You are assaulted by a drunk on the streets: Did he punch hard enough to hurt, or was it only mild impact? Did anything happen worthy of counter-action, or nothing? Your partner yells at you: at first you are taken aback, but did it actually hurt, or was it only emotional impact?—and if it did hurt, did it do any damage, or was it only pain? If only pain, it will subside soon, and you can move on. We do not have to react to everything as an injury.

One of the great benefits of the Buddha's analysis of experience is that we become aware that there are two kinds of feeling, one primary and one secondary. The primary one will be something like impact, raw pleasure, raw pain, but in our ordinary experience it will seem inseparable from an additional layer of feeling that magnifies it. You taste a marvelous new wine, and immediately feel that a civilized life is impossible without it. You dance with someone really attractive who seems to like you, and for days afterwards your days and nights are plagued with lascivious fantasies because surely something more is meant to happen. Or someone shoves you, so you react with indignation and rage, and shove back. You slip on ice and crash to the ground; immediately you are trembling with shock and dismay, your body hurts, and from then on you never want to venture outside in the cold again. You want to be a writer, but after several days working on a short story you finally dare to show it to a respected friend, who laughs —so, mortally wounded, you never write another word for twenty years and dedicate all your spare time to reading novels or watching TV.

In all of these cases there is a first feeling that is simple, but it manifests to us as packaged in a more complex feeling that gives the first feeling more significance than it really has. The Buddha illuminates this beautifully in the *Parable of the Arrow*:

> The Blessed One said, "When touched with a feeling of pain, the uninstructed run-of-the-mill person sorrows, grieves, and laments, beats his breast, becomes distraught. So he feels two pains, physical and mental. Just as if they were to shoot a man with an arrow and, right afterward, were to shoot him with another one, so that he would feel the pains of two arrows; in the same way, when touched with a feeling of pain, the [Normal Joe] sorrows, grieves, and laments, beats his breast, becomes distraught. So he feels two pains, physical and mental.
>
> "As he is touched by that painful feeling, he is resistant.

Any resistance-obsession with regard to that painful feeling obsesses him. Touched by that painful feeling, he delights in sensual pleasure. Why is that? Because the uninstructed run-of-the-mill person does not discern any escape from painful feeling aside from sensual pleasure. As he is delighting in sensual pleasure, any passion-obsession with regard to that feeling of pleasure obsesses him. He does not discern, as it actually is present, the origination, passing away, allure, drawback, or escape from that feeling. As he does not discern the origination, passing away, allure, drawback, or escape from that feeling, then any ignorance-obsession with regard to that feeling of neither-pleasure-nor-pain obsesses him.

"Sensing a feeling of pleasure, he senses it as though joined with it. Sensing a feeling of pain, he senses it as though joined with it. Sensing a feeling of neither-pleasure-nor-pain, he senses it as though joined with it. This is called a an uninstructed run-of-the-mill person joined with birth, aging, and death; with sorrows, lamentations, pains, distresses, and despairs. He is joined, I tell you, with suffering and stress.

"Now, the well-instructed disciple of the noble ones, when touched with a feeling of pain, does not sorrow, grieve, or lament, does not beat his breast or become distraught. So he feels one pain: physical, but not mental. Just as if they were to shoot a man with an arrow and, right afterward, did not shoot him with another one, so that he would feel the pain of only one arrow. In the same way, when touched with a feeling of pain, the well-instructed disciple of the noble ones does not sorrow, grieve, or lament, does not beat his breast or become distraught. He feels one pain: physical, but not mental." [1]

---

[1] Thanissaro Bhikkhu (trans.), "Sallatha Sutta," *Samyutta Nikaya* 36.6. Access to Insight, 1997 www.accesstoinsight.org/lib/authors/sn36.006.than.html.

The first arrow is the simple primary feeling, but then we shoot an extra arrow at ourselves, or even an entire assortment of arrows. With experience, and the habit of paying attention to what we are really feeling, we start to see that even though most of our feelings present themselves to us as "natural" and inevitable, they are usually compounds of more than one arrow, and the only one we have to manage is the first. The secondary feelings are not intrinsic to the experience. We may get upset at being punched in the head by the drunk on the street, but when we realize that in boxing class we actually rather enjoyed being punched in the head, and that boxers even look forward to such assaults, we see that upset and rage are not intrinsic to being punched. Similarly, we may feel arousal and desire on being seated next to a physically attractive person—but when we think about how many objectively pretty people we have become indifferent to because of their shallow conversation or spiteful behavior, we see that there is nothing intrinsically erotic about anybody's appearance. Even with the death of loved ones, we know that some cultures and individuals celebrate the passing into a better life, or rejoice in the satisfying completion of a life, or find relief in deliverance from chronic pain and indignity: even sorrow is not intrinsic to death.

The *Parable of the Arrow* can save us from unnecessary emotional drama and also obfuscation. There is genuine feeling, and extraneous or extrinsic feeling. When we are able to discriminate between the two, we can respond rather than react. Rather than becoming lost in a mixed cloud of emotions that all press upon us as urgent and essential, we can feel more clearly what is primary and not be bullied by adventitious compulsions.

Once in the ocean off Penang I was stung by a Portuguese Man-O'-War. The tentacle wrapped around my right arm, and it felt like a massive electric shock. As I pulled away, realizing what had happened, I carefully detached the virulent thread and watched my arm swelling and turning black. The initial shock subsided quickly as I reasoned that I was unlikely to die or lose the use of my arm. Instead, it was extremely interesting to observe the change in the sensation over the weeks: it was novel, and gave me a new appreciation for my arm. There were two things I had always been curious about in the natural world: what it would feel like to be shocked by an electric eel or stung by a big deadly jellyfish. Now I had met one of them. It was painful, yes, but something wonderful and nothing to complain about; besides, the black spiral line around my arm entertained my friends for months afterwards.

One of the Buddha's most memorable analogies is given in the *Potthapada Sutta*, and it is so powerful that it causes Citta the son of an elephant trainer to leap for joy, and then renounce everything to join the Buddha. The context for this analogy is a sometimes abstruse conversation with Potthapada, a Brahmin of highly scholastic inclinations who seems to share a more general Hindu anxiety about the persistence of *Atman* (Self/Soul) and about elevated spiritual states. Citta has accompanied Potthapada in the second half of the Sutta, and has just asked a question about whether there is any underlying continuity of the Self/Soul from one stage to another of a person's development. In other words, does the Self/Soul persist the same from one moment to another? Startlingly, the Buddha responds with this analogy:

> Just as in the case of cow's milk—from the milk come curds, from the curds come butter, from the butter comes ghee, and from the ghee comes the cream of ghee. Whenever there is milk, at that time, one does not refer to it as "curds," nor as "butter," nor as "ghee," nor as the "cream of ghee." At that time, one refers to it only as "milk." And whenever there are curds, at that time, one does not refer to them as "milk," nor as "butter," nor as "ghee," nor as the "cream of ghee." At that time, one refers to them only as "curds." Whenever there is butter, at that time, one does not refer to it as "milk," nor as "curds," nor as "ghee," nor as the "cream of ghee." At that time, one refers to it only as "butter." Whenever there is ghee, at that time, one does not refer to it as "milk," nor as "curds," nor as "butter," nor as the "cream of ghee." At that time, one refers to it only as "ghee." Whenever there is the "cream of ghee," at that

time, one does not refer to it as "milk," nor as "curds," nor as "butter," nor as "ghee." At that time, one refers to it only as the "cream of ghee." [1]

The repetitiveness of the style is not mere pedantry: we are being asked to slow down and behold with our mind's eye milk, curds, butter, ghee, and cream of ghee, and not rush to a theoretical summation. Contemplate these: the taste, color, texture, smell—how interestingly different they are (such that a person can love milk but dislike curds), how each is its own delicious dish, yet how each so astonishingly comes from the white liquid produced by a cow for her calf. This contemplation becomes even more vivid if one brings in the vast range of things we call "cheese." The common manner of referring to curds and butter as "curds" and "butter" rather than "the curd phase of milk" or "the butter phase of milk" ("buttermilk" is different!) points to an unavoidable truth: there is no such thing as "milk" that persists through all of these, and if you look you will not be able to show it to me. The curds came from milk, and now curds are simply what they are: curds, not milk. Looking closely, you will not find a particle that is in between curds and milk, but it will be curds *or* milk. If there is an in-between, it will be its own thing, such as kefir; and it might be possible to make an in-between by, say, mixing butter and milk, but that too will be its own thing, not just a form of milk. In the realm of natural transformation, change occurs over time and is conditioned by such things as temperature, microbial life, light, oxygen. The thing changing cannot be pulled out and separated from these conditions, which are in fact infinite (including the conditions of physics and chemistry for there to be a planet with microbial life), and because of this inseparability a thing may be fundamentally indis-

---

[1] "Potthapada Sutta," *Early Buddhist Discourses*, John J. Holder, trans., (Cambridge, 2006) 148.

tinguishable from its conditions. This does not mean they are the *same* as their conditions, because obviously butter is not simply the same as all its antecedents. Each change is thoroughgoing from one moment to the next, and there is never any *thing* that can be shown to underlie the different moments. Curds, butter, ghee are different *moments* of what was once milk, but not different manifestations *of* milk. They are also not really fixed things themselves, because the conditions that make them up are in constant flux; yet the fact that they are in flux doesn't necessarily make them unintelligible, because there are clearly patterns and regularities to this change. The analogy doesn't deny the validity of calling these moments milk, curds, butter, and so on, or the validity of saying that they come from cow's milk: from a conventional standpoint, it is correct to do so, and incorrect to claim that because everything is in flux there is really nothing present.

> But such as these are only popular expressions, ordinary language, common ways of speaking, common designations, which the Tathagatha uses without being led astray.[2]

The constant process of transformation, amid infinite conditions, is the way in which curds and butter can come to be from milk; and indeed if there were no ceaseless transformation there would be no curds or butter. Even if we strive to halt the process by killing all the microbes in the milk, sooner or later even sterilized milk will change; indeed, sterilized milk is itself a moment of what was once milk, conditioned by sterilizing and sterilizers. At each moment there is something that comes to be through and in transformation, because nothing in our experience remains static and immune to change. The universe flows—or, as the Japanese Zen philosopher Dogen likes to put it, the mountains are walking.

---

[2] "Potthapada Sutta," *Early Buddhist Discourses*, 169.

The Buddha doesn't interpret the analogy to mean that there is no Self/Soul. Rather, while there may be no *thing* underlying these various conditioned forms that started as milk, there is a phenomenal continuity that enables us to categorize them as moments of what was once milk. These moments are what it *means* to be milk, for only milk can change into curds, butter, and ghee under specific conditions. The implications are momentous.

What am I? Do I even need to be preoccupied with a *what* that I must be? When I am with my parents, I am all child; with my children, I am all parent; with my spouse, all spouse—and at work, wholly absorbed in the work. When I go to the gym, I work out to win and play with all my heart; and after the gym, I can be swept away by a piano sonata and moved to tears. Of course this is on a good day; on a bad day, I am thinking about work while playing with the kids, or worried about my aging parents while at work. Yet even on a bad day, I am whole in my division; that is to say, sitting at my desk and worrying about my parents is itself a whole distractedness, and I am occupying the distraction wholly. In each activity I become a different moment of what at the beginning of the day was a groggy person stumbling to the bathroom. It is amazing how thoroughgoing the transformations are. My children would be surprised at how I am with my parents, and vice versa; neither parents nor children can imagine me studying the "Potthapada Sutta," and many people who study such texts with me cannot really picture me climbing playground equipment with my daughter. All these transformations would be impossible if we had an unchanging underlying self that we hauled around like a boulder in the belly. We can live as if we had a boulder in the belly, and sadly we usually do— but what a wonder it is that I can flow so wholeheartedly and seamlessly into each one of these moments of myself. It is a miracle that from the teat of a cow there comes milk that can transform into curds, butter, ghee, and cream of ghee—and into me when I digest it. This is why the elephant trainer's son jumps for joy when he understands the analogy: the boulder of Atman has been rolled away.

23. *"Venerable Gotama, Is There A Soul?"*

This may be the most burning question for seekers who come to the Buddha from religions built on belief in imperishable individual souls or in a single omnipresent, eternal Soul. One of the most memorable exchanges on this question is initiated by a Brahmin wanderer named Vacchagotta, who in various suttas is featured as an expert in big speculative questions. The conversation begins enigmatically:

> "Venerable Gotama, is there a self?"
> When this was said, the Blessed One was silent.
> "Then is there no self?"
> A second time, the Blessed One was silent.[1]

The word "self" translates *atta* (in Sanskrit, *atman*), and is one of those immensely rich, resonant words that have provoked thousands of years of debate and discussion. For human beings and other sentient beings *atta* means "the innermost self" or "soul," the living core that is immortal, persisting through time and perhaps even residing outside of time. When we speak loosely of the "self" of a world, a culture, a landscape, a mountain, we also mean the underlying essence that unites the varying appearances into "one thing." Today I saw a murmuration of starlings squabbling with a flock of robins, noticed that the red leaves on my flowering pear tree have started to turn brown, needed to wear my thickest wool coat, and found feathery frost

---

[1] Thanissaro Bhikkhu (trans.)," Ananda Sutta: To Ananda," *Samyutta Nikaya* 44:10, Access to Insight, 2004. http://www.access-toinsight.org/tipitaka/sn/sn44/sn44.010.than.html.

on my car window: all these bespeak a "self" of winter, which had suddenly arrived, ousting autumn, and which cannot be experienced directly but through signs.

When we point to ourselves to say "it's me," we know that the Me we are referring to cannot be pointed at, cannot be pulled out and displayed: my finger points physically to my jacket, or, when that is removed, to my shirt, or to my t-shirt under it, or to my chest, but none of these observable things is what I mean by Me. My Self underlies all of the phenomena associated with me and cannot be pointed to. My clothes, my body, my actions, my CV, are all a metonymy for something that exists in supposition as their substratum. Vacchagotta asks if this substratum exists—if there is an "I" or not, if there is a unifying Soul, or am I nothing but a temporary aggregation of parts that are themselves temporary aggregations of parts, all changing from moment to moment?

The Buddha's silence might be taken as either a refusal to answer Vacchagotta's questions, or as the only appropriate answer. To understand this, let's look at how the Buddha talks about the self in the "Anatta-Lakhana Sutta" (*Samyutta Nikaya* 22:59), which was the Buddha's second teaching, given to the five monks who were his best friends at the time. Coming just seven weeks after his enlightenment, the teaching is charged with the electricity of new discovery:

> Thus I heard. On one occasion the Blessed One was living at Benares, in the Deer Park at Isipatana (the Resort of Seers). There he addressed the bhikkhus of the group of five: "Bhikkhus." — "Venerable sir," they replied. The Blessed One said this.
> "Bhikkhus, form is not-self. Were form self, then this form would not lead to affliction, and one could have it of form: 'Let my form be thus, let my form be not thus.' And since form is not-self, so it leads to affliction, and none can

have it of form: 'Let my form be thus, let my form be not thus.'

"Bhikkhus, feeling is not-self...[formulaic phrasing above repeated]

"Bhikkhus, perception is not-self...

"Bhikkhus, determinations are not-self...

"Bhikkhus, consciousness is not self. Were consciousness self, then this consciousness would not lead to affliction, and one could have it of consciousness: 'Let my consciousness be thus, let my consciousness be not thus.' And since consciousness is not-self, so it leads to affliction, and none can have it of consciousness: 'Let my consciousness be thus, let my consciousness be not thus.'

"Bhikkhus, how do you conceive it: is form permanent or impermanent?" — "Impermanent, venerable Sir." — "Now is what is impermanent painful or pleasant?" — "Painful, venerable Sir." — "Now is what is impermanent, what is painful since subject to change, fit to be regarded thus: 'This is mine, this is I, this is my self'"? — "No, venerable sir."

"Is feeling permanent or impermanent?...

"Is perception permanent or impermanent?...

"Are determinations permanent or impermanent?...

"Is consciousness permanent or impermanent?" — "Impermanent, venerable sir." — "Now what is impermanent pleasant or painful?" — "Painful, venerable sir." — "Now is what is impermanent, what is painful since subject to change, fit to be regarded thus: 'This is mine, this is I, this is my self'"? — "No, venerable sir."

"So, bhikkhus any kind of form whatever, whether past, future or presently arisen, whether gross or subtle, whether in oneself or external, whether inferior or superior, whether far or near, must with right understanding how it is, be regarded thus: 'This is not mine, this is not I, this is not myself.'

"Any kind of feeling whatever...

"Any kind of perception whatever...
"Any kind of determination whatever...
"Any kind of consciousness whatever, whether past, future or presently arisen, whether gross or subtle, whether in oneself or external, whether inferior or superior, whether far or near must, with right understanding how it is, be regarded thus: 'This is not mine, this is not I, this is not my self.'[2]

Rather than just telling us how it is, the Buddha is giving us a framework of questions for self- interrogation. If there is a "self," where does it exist, and can we find it anywhere? Of the possible wheres, there are only five: the five *kandhas*, "heaps" or agglomerations, which constitute the entirety of our beings. These are 1) bodily "form"; 2) the "feelings" of pain, pleasure, or neither, which accompany every sensation; 3) "perception" or what we sense with our sense organs, including our organ of internal perception, the mind; 4) "determination," which includes volition, predispositions, preferential tendencies, all the aspects connected with willing and choosing that have given our existences direction and that establish inertia for the future; and 5) "consciousness," the dimension of thought, intellection, and awareness. There is no other *kandha*. All five have been compared to five heaps thrown together to make a single being, or the confluence of five rivers rushing together. If the self can be found anywhere, it must be in the *kandhas*.

With characteristic methodical thoroughness, the Buddha then works through the *kandhas* one by one. Am I my body? If

---

[2] Ñanamoli Thera(trans.), "Anatta-lakkhana Sutta: The Discourse on the Not-self Characteristic," *Samyutta Nikaya* 22:59, Access to Insight, 1993. http://www.accesstoinsight.org/tipitaka/sn/sn22/sn22.059.nymo.html.

our selves were the same as our bodies, we would never be at odds with our bodies; instead, we struggle with our bodily limitations, with the frequency of disease and physical pain, with aging, and with death. There is always tension between us and our bodies. But am I my feelings, am I my perceptions? Am I my desires? If not, then am I my thoughts, my consciousness? It turns out that the self cannot be found in the other four *kandhas*: we struggle with our likes, dislikes, and neutralities, and are often surprised and appalled by our feelings; we can resist perceptions, and also be confused by our perceptions; we can suffer conflicting volitions and be paralyzed in dilemmas, and we are capable of not wanting what we want; we can make serious mistakes in our thoughts and judgments, and can repudiate states of mind and mental commitments that have until then dominated our sense of reality. Our inability to identify simply with any of the *kandhas* proves that the self is not to be found in them, and therefore not to be found in all of them taken together.

The Buddha then points out that in our experience, all five *kandhas* are subject to change and are constantly in motion. Every cell in our body changes moment by moment, the temperature and blood pressure vary, all the fluids are in motion, and the content of the blood changes in accordance with what we have eaten and with the capacity of the whole organism to digest. The body at least contrives to stay stable and recognizable from day to day, even though philosophers have been quick to dismiss the body for being mired in flux. The sensations, feelings, and volitions are much more volatile and harder to pin down than the body— and what can be less stable, more entirely in motion, than consciousness? It is barely possible to keep track, in the space of a day, of all our states of consciousness—not just the moods and emotions, but also the thoughts, the things that catch our attention, the preoccupations and vexations. Impermanence is what we experience in all the "heaps" of our being—but what we are looking for is that thing whereby we can be considered "ourselves," something that continues selfsame from one moment to the next, unchangingly itself underneath the chaos. We do not experience this thing in any of the five *kandhas*, and there is no sixth *kandha*.

There is a lot to unpack and chew over in the Buddha's laconic, repetitive formulations. The careful search for the self amidst the *kandhas* is itself a form of focused meditation, but in this search one of the things we notice is that in fact the self cannot be an object of the search. Instead, what we call "self" is a process of self-making, a continuous activity in which identification is constantly being attempted. Regarding our bodies, for instance, think of all those times we reject photographs of ourselves that "don't look like us" and settle on the one that is "us," that is worthy of representing us; or, more interestingly, consider the person who cannot accept *any* photograph of themselves as a good likeness. The act of picking out a good picture of myself exists in the context of a lifelong and developing process of making an image of myself that I wish—for many complex reasons—to identify with. What goes on when we choose and reject an image of ourselves is worthy of patient investigation. While we settle on a presentable, official image, we can also at the same time rejoice in the lover who delights in our unofficial morning face and morning hair, and we can feel pleasure when a small nephew fondly plays with our grey hair or strokes our bald patch. We are caught here in a web of sometimes contradictory identifications; it can be consternating when our lover who adores our middle-aged frailty thinks that our favorite picture of ourselves is slightly silly and not like us at all. With feelings, volitions, and thoughts, the activity of seeking something to identify with goes on automatically and at a much deeper level. When we are angry, in love, or feeling righteous, we identify so wholly with those states that it is impossible to see ourselves objectively, and when even close friends disagree with us then, we feel that it is our selves that are under attack. It is possible to feel anger, love, and righteousness in succession—and then the identification with three sets of thoughts and emotions can lead perplexingly in different directions. In an important conversation with the beloved disciple Ananda, the Buddha takes on again the identification with feeling:

> "In what ways, Ānanda, does one considering (the idea of) self consider it? One considering (the idea of) self either considers feeling as self, saying: 'Feeling is my self.' Or he considers: 'Feeling is not my self; my self is without experience of feeling.' Or he considers: 'Feeling is not my self, but my self is not without experience of feeling. My self feels; for my self is subject to feeling.'
>
> "Therein, Ānanda, the one who says 'Feeling is my self' should be asked: 'Friend, there are these three kinds of feeling—pleasant feeling, painful feeling, and neither-painful-nor-pleasant feeling. Of these three kinds of feeling, which do you consider as self?'
>
> "Ānanda, on the occasion when one experiences a pleasant feeling one does not, on that same occasion, experience a painful feeling or a neither-painful-nor-pleasant feeling; on that occasion one experiences only a pleasant feeling. On the occasion when one experiences a painful feeling one does not, on that same occasion, experience a pleasant feeling or a neither-painful-nor-pleasant feeling; on that occasion one experiences only a painful feeling. On the occasion when one experiences a neither-painful-nor-pleasant feeling one does not, on that same occasion, experience a pleasant feeling or a painful feeling; on that occasion one experiences only a neither-painful-nor-pleasant feeling.
>
> "Ānanda, pleasant feeling is impermanent, conditioned, dependently arisen, subject to destruction, falling away,

fading out, and ceasing. Painful feeling is impermanent, conditioned, dependently arisen, subject to destruction, falling away, fading out, and ceasing. Neither-painful-nor-pleasant feeling is impermanent, conditioned, dependently arisen, subject to destruction, falling away, fading out, and ceasing.

"If, when experiencing a pleasant feeling, one thinks: 'This is my self,' then with the ceasing of that pleasant feeling one thinks: 'My self has disappeared.' If, when experiencing a painful feeling, one thinks: 'This is my self,' then with the ceasing of that painful feeling one thinks: 'My self has disappeared.' If, when experiencing a neither-painful-nor-pleasant feeling, one thinks: 'This is my self,' then with the ceasing of that neither-painful-nor-pleasant feeling one thinks: 'My self has disappeared.'

"Thus one who says 'Feeling is my self' considers as self something which, even here and now, is impermanent, a mixture of pleasure and pain, and subject to arising and falling away. Therefore, Ānanda, because of this it is not acceptable to consider: 'Feeling is my self.'

"Ānanda, the one who says 'Feeling is not my self, my self is without experience of feeling'—he should be asked: 'Friend, where there is nothing at all that is felt, could the idea "I am" occur there?'"

"Certainly not, venerable sir."

"Therefore, Ānanda, because of this it is not acceptable to consider: 'Feeling is not my self; my self is without experience of feeling.'

"Ānanda, the one who says 'Feeling is not my self, but my self is not without experience of feeling. My self feels; for my self is subject to feeling'—he should be asked: 'Friend, if feeling were to cease absolutely and utterly without remainder, then, in the complete absence of feeling, with the cessation of feeling, could (the idea) "I am this" occur there?'"

"Certainly not, venerable sir."

"Therefore, Ānanda, because of this it is not acceptable to consider: 'Feeling is not my self, but my self is not without experience of feeling. My self feels; for my self is subject to feeling.'

"Ānanda, when a bhikkhu does not consider feeling as self, and does not consider self as without experience of feeling, and does not consider: 'My self feels; for my self is subject to feeling'—then, being without such considerations, he does not cling to anything in the world. Not clinging, he is not agitated. Not being agitated, he personally attains nibbāna. He understands: 'Destroyed is birth, the holy life has been lived, what had to be done has been done, there is no returning to this state of being.'"[3]

In brief, if I seek to identify my self in my feelings, which feelings do I fix on for identification? If it is the happy me, am I not myself when miserable? If my self is to be found in my pain, then am I not myself when in pleasure? Furthermore, any feeling of pain or pleasure is changing all the time, so in what part of them can I find myself? If I reject this and say that the self exists beyond feeling, unfeeling and therefore unfelt, why would I have any cause to look for the self anywhere, since experientially it is nothing to me? Only when the seeker stops trying to locate and objectify the self—both in feelings and in non-feeling—will he attain freedom from agitation. The agitation itself is caused by the futile attempt to solidify the self, whether as individual ego or as world-soul, which is an amplification of ego; the way out of this agitation begins with being able to catch ourselves in the act of making identifications.

In all of this, the Buddha is making no assertions about the

[3] Bhikkhu Bodhi (trans.), "Mahanidana Sutta: The Great Causes Discourse," *Digha Nikaya* 15, SuttaCentral. https://suttacentral.net/en/dn15.

existence of the self; he wants us to essay, to make an empirical inquiry into our experience of selfing, and to understand for ourselves in what way there is or isn't a self. What we see is a continual process of identifying, of making selves—never unitary even in a single person. If this is what the word "self" means, then there is a self; but if the object sought for in identification is an eternal selfsameness from moment to moment, then we do not find it anywhere in any experience we can point to. He does not say this version of self doesn't exist, just that we don't find it anywhere except in the imagination of faith, which is also not simple non-existence. The more pressing question is why we are looking for the self, what is at stake when we want it to exist or not exist.

To return now to the Brahmin wanderer Vacchagotta, the Buddha denies him a straightforward yes or no, and also a complicated explanation: he answers with silence, partly to throw Vacchagotta back onto himself and provoke him to question his question, but partly to show to this clever quibbler that to such questions there really is no answer. Non-questions get non-answers. It is comparable to someone who watches *Star Wars* and asks afterwards if the world of the film was real or not. This is a non-question, because clearly in some way the world of the film was real enough to be experienced by us: dreams and fantasies have existence as dreams and fantasies, and have more power to affect our lives than gross material things like chairs and tables—which also came from somebody's imagination. Vacchagotta's non-question is generated by attachment to the need to reduce all experience to one simple thing that can be given a definition. A genuine question would be something like, "In what *way* is the world of *Star Wars* real or not real, true or not true?" The answers to this will be more intelligent and nuanced.

Then Vacchagotta the wanderer got up from his seat and left.

Then, not long after Vacchagotta the wanderer had left, Ven. Ananda said to the Blessed One, "Why, lord, did the Blessed One not answer when asked a question by Vacchagotta the wanderer?"

"Ananda, if I — being asked by Vacchagotta the wanderer if there is a self — were to answer that there is a self, that would be conforming with those brahmans & contemplatives who are exponents of eternalism [the view that there is an eternal, unchanging soul]. If I — being asked by Vacchagotta the wanderer if there is no self — were to answer that there is no self, that would be conforming with those brahmans & contemplatives who are exponents of annihilationism [the view that death is the annihilation of consciousness]. If I — being asked by Vacchagotta the wanderer if there is a self — were to answer that there is a self, would that be in keeping with the arising of knowledge that all phenomena are not-self?"

"No, lord."

"And if I — being asked by Vacchagotta the wanderer if there is no self — were to answer that there is no self, the bewildered Vacchagotta would become even more bewildered: 'Does the self I used to have now not exist?'"[4]

Answering yes would corroborate Vacchagotta's predisposition to hold to an eternal self, which we don't find in experience of the *skandhas*; answering no would corroborate him in his deep-seated anxiety that then nothing really exists. These theoretical positions are solidifications, congealments, of the more dynamic ways for self to be or not be. The self happens like the forming of a bubble, like the making of a dream, real in a way, and not real in another way: the point is not to recite this as a

---

[4] Thanissaro Bhikkhu, "Ananda butta: To Ananda."

striking philosophical paradox, but to be able to see selfing as it happens and to live it in its real unreality, its unreal reality.

24. Dog on a Leash

"Fasting," said a good friend who happened to be in the midst of a fast, "is a good way to confront the ego and reach the limits of its control." Even in a more gentle fast, where a modicum of food is permitted for mere sustenance, and where one knows with rational clarity that there is no danger of death or even harmful emaciation, one experiences in the first two days the whole range of emotional resistance from discomfort to panicked desperation as the necessities for physical survival are systematically withdrawn. In a more drastic fast, with only fruit juice allowed, I have felt something like terror as my digestive tract was brought to growling, screaming depletion. We hardly ever feel hungry, and are distressed if we have to miss a meal. Rationally considered, the distress cannot be intrinsic to the act of missing a meal, since there are other times—for example, during illness, or after the surfeit of gluttonous festivity—when missing a meal might even feel good. Regularity in feeding brings profound emotional solace: the idea of an unending supply not only of food, but of food we like, reassures us against extinction itself and against the extinction of our individual selves. It safeguards our ego or *jiva*—and when the food is denied, we are brought to the edge of our ego, as to the edge of an abyss. Of course, rational reflection pulls us back and comforts us: no one we know has actually perished of fasting, we are in the good hands of our spiritual group, we have done this before and been fine, and so on.

If you have ever attempted a reading fast, you will know that it is not only physical inanition that can take us to the brink of primal desperation. Just as food and drink are nutriments for the body, so also thoughts, perceptions, experiences, and words are nutriments to the consciousness. Try a reading fast. For one week, you are not allowed to read books, magazines, newspapers, web pages, advertisements, emails, social media posts; you are also not allowed to read the information on food packets or toiletries—so at the breakfast table, do not let your eyes wander mechanically to the cereal box. On the first day you will experience various levels of resistance: first, after a few hours of restlessness, you will try to rationalize your way out of the fast, telling yourself you already know what is going to happen or that the whole thing is a pointless exercise; then there will be a period of desperate emptiness, as if coming out of severe addiction, and if you stay with this, you will feel something like terror, as if consciousness itself were being starved to nothingness. Any person who has not cultivated a rich mental life will be close to going out of his mind after a day of this, but the lifelong reader will have stores of words and thoughts packed in the memory— volumes and volumes of distraction from the emptiness. But sooner or later one can feel even that running dry—at which point the resourceful reader will start to write books, invent original geometry proofs, think up novels. We will do anything but let the mental production grind to a halt. Even if we never get so far, it may be enough to realize how compulsive reading can be; and that even if reading may not be our particular way to feed the mind, we all have a favored strategy to guarantee a constant stream of nutriment to our consciousness. If this stream is staunched or dries up, we find ourselves thrashing for breath like a fish on dry land.

When we reach that edge and are about to pull back, it is good to linger there a little and look at what it is. In any kind of fasting we are tempted to view this moment as an obstacle we need to move through in order to get to the state of lucid contentment that follows it—but it may be that our dread and panic tell us more about who we are and that we need to listen carefully to the uncomfortable.

Buried deep in the vast collection of discourses known as the *Samyutta Nikaya*, there are two versions of a potent little parable called "The Leash" (or the *Gaddula Sutta*). In this parable the Buddha gives us an image of ourselves in our normal "chained" state, where we can never stray too far from a sturdy central post:

> "Suppose, bhikkhus, a dog tied up on a leash was bound to a strong post or pillar: it would just keep on running and revolving around that same post or pillar. So too, the uninstructed worldling ... regards form as self ... feeling as self ... perception as self ... volitional formations as self ... consciousness as self.... He just keeps running and revolving around form, around feeling, around perception, around volitional formations, around consciousness. As he keeps on running and revolving around them, he is not freed from form, not freed from feeling, not freed from perception, not freed from volitional formations, not freed from consciousness. He is not freed from birth, aging, and death; not freed from sorrow, lamentation, pain, displeasure, and despair; not freed from suffering, I say."[1]

The body (form), feelings, perceptions, volitions, and consciousness are the "aggregates" or heaps that constitute who we are: we are nothing but them, and they are constantly moving and changing, constantly mutually conditioning, without any ultimate spatial or temporal boundary. The problem is that we identify them as our self, we identify with them, and this act of identification—which asserts a solid core in the middle of the tornado—is our leashing to the immoveable post of a conceived self. The post is the idea of a self, the leash is the idea-ing of

---

[1] Bhikkhu Bodhi (trans.), *Gaddula Suttas*, *Samyutta Nikaya* 22.99, SuttaCentral. https://suttacentral.net/en/sn22.99.

self—and our running around the post is our way of consolidating circle and radius by the repetitious attachments with which we make our selves.

The second version of this Sutta emphasizes how close we stay to the post:

> "Suppose, bhikkhus, a dog tied up on a leash was bound to a strong post or pillar. If it walks, it walks close to that post or pillar. If it stands, it stands close to that post or pillar. If it sits down, it sits down close to that post or pillar. If it lies down, it lies down close to that post or pillar." [2]

The radius is tiny, for we confine ourselves to our familiar little circle—and this precisely is the foundation of our unhappiness. The Buddha will then go on to describe how through discipline the Buddhist practitioner frees himself from leash and post, but in this essay I want to dwell more on the range of this leash. What do we experience when we pull hard and reach the end of the leash?

The twentieth-century Italian philosopher Julius Evola expands on the Parable of the Leash in his strange, rich book on the Pali suttas, *The Doctrine of Awakening* (1943; English, 1948). Evola sees the modern human being as self-imprisoned in a materialist, external orientation to his own life, lost in the illusion of infinite "options" and not capable of seeing more deeply than the merely psychological. Even so, we all experience moments when the reassuring solidity of what we take to be real dissolves suddenly into blackness:

> [T]he life [modern man] normally leads is as if outside himself; half sleepwalking, he moves between psychological reflexes and images that hide from him the deepest and

---

[2] Bhikkhu Bodhi (trans.), "The Leash 2", *Samyutta Nikaya* 22:100, SuttaCentral <https://suttacentral.net/en/sn22.99>

most fearful substance of existence. Only in particular circumstances is the veil of what is, fundamentally, a providential illusion torn aside. For example, in all moments of sudden danger, on the point of being threatened either by the vanishing of ground from under one's feet through the opening of a chasm or glacier crevasse, or in touching inadvertently a glowing coal or an electrified object, an instantaneous reaction takes place. This reaction does not proceed from the "will, consciousness, nor from the "I" since this part follows only after the initial reaction is complete; in the first moment it is preceded by something more profound, more rapid, and more absolute. During extreme hunger, panic, fear, sensual craving, or extreme pain and terror the same force again shows itself—and he who can comprehend it directly in these moments likewise creates for himself the faculty of perceiving it gradually as the invisible substratum of all waking life. The subterranean roots of inclinations, faiths, atavisms, of invincible and irrational convictions, habits, and character, all that lives as animality, as biological race, all the urges of the body—all this goes back to the same principle. Compared with it, the "will of the I" has, normally, a liberty equivalent to that of a dog tied to a fairly long chain that he does not notice until he has passed a certain limit. If one goes beyond that limit, the profound force is not slow to awaken, either to supplant the "I" or to mislead it, making it believe that it wills that which, in fact, the force itself wills. The wild force of imagination and of suggestion takes us to the same point: to that where according to the so-called law of "converse effort," one does something the more strongly the more one "wills" against it—as sleep eludes one the more one "wills" it, or as the suggestion that one will fall into an abyss will certainly cause one to fall if one "wills" against it.

This force, which is connected with the emotive and irrational energies, gradually identifies itself as the very force that rules the profound functions of physical life, over

which the "will," the "mind, and the "I" have very little influence, to which they are external and on which they live
parasitically, extracting the essential fluids yet without having to go down for them into the heart of the trunk. Thus
one must ask oneself: What, of this "my" body, can be jus-
tifiably thought of as subject to "my will? Do "I" will "my"
breath or the mixtures of the digestive juices by which food
is digested? Do "I" will my form, my flesh, or my being this
man who is conditioned thus and not otherwise? Can he
who asks himself this not go on even further and ask himself: My "will" itself, my consciousness, my "I"—do I will
these, or simply is it that they are?[3]

This is the vision that lies on the other side of fasting,
which is a way of easing us towards the realization. Faced with
this, and made uneasy by it, the sages of the Upanishads would
perform sacrifices: the world devours, all beings devour and are
devoured, we are the devouring, and the devouring is us; life is
nothing but nutriment, digestive combustion as well as intellectual conflagration, birth and sustaining and destruction on every
level all at the same time. There is no way to change all this, but
there may be a way out if we ever find ourselves at the point
where we cannot take it any more—yet the way out is not to escape with ourselves intact, for that would be wanting to bring
leash and post with us. It involves learning to "comprehend it
directly," as Evola puts it, not just theoretically; and to "create"
for ourselves *the faculty of perceiving it gradually as the invisible
substratum of all waking life.* And the greatest masters of such
comprehension might not be the conventional spiritual teachers,
but writers like Chekhov, Kafka, and Beckett.

---

[3] Julius Evola, *The Doctrine of Awakening*, 1995/96, pp.54-55
<https://archive.org/details/TheDoctrineOfAwakening>

I am employed by the parish, and do my duty to the point
where it is almost too much for one man. Though badly
paid, I am generous and helpful to the poor. I should like
to see Rosa provided for, and then the boy may have his
way as far as I'm concerned, and I shall be ready to die as
well. What am I doing in this endless winter! [4]

---

[4] Franz Kafka, "A Country Doctor," translated by Michael Hoff-
man, London Review of Books. http://thespace.lrb.co.uk/article/a-
country-doctor-by-franz-kafka-translated-by-michael-hofmann/.

Part 3

Two Masterpieces

The Pali Discourses of the Buddha are, in general, strikingly barren of literary beauty and poetic subtlety. The language tends to be plodding, methodical, dry, uniform, and repetitive—as if the writers of this vast body of work had deliberately vowed to reject all possibility of verbal pleasure and seduction, presenting the student instead with something that often feels like a relentless instruction manual. The foundational books of other traditions abound with passages of poetic richness: for example, the Upanishads, the Bible, Confucius and Mencius, and Zhuangzi. Charismatic teachers owe much of their attraction and influence to a gift for memorable expression; it is unlikely that the Buddha would have attracted such a large and devoted following if his characteristic manner of speaking were as stern, abstract, and desiccated as it is portrayed in the Pali Canon. The writers of the Suttas ruthlessly defoliated the words of the Buddha of all grace and charm, and created a sort of anti-literature that has a strange power to delight and shock even through its austere avoidance of stylistic beautification and emotional appeals. As with the Haiku writings of 17th century Japan, the Buddha's discourses are beautiful because they strenuously shun the beautiful: after all, deserts are beautiful because they are deserts. Among the Suttas, however, there are two remarkable literary masterpieces: "On Ratthapala," which is almost a dark comedy of manners, and "Fruits of the Homeless Life," which is almost a Greek tragedy.

25. A Summary of the Buddha's Teachings: Ratthapala, Part 1

The Sutta *On Ratthapala* falls into two distinct halves, of which the first gives the rich dramatic context to the second, where ostensibly the main teaching occurs. I'll begin with the "teaching" half and then swing back to the narration of the first half to see how it both galvanizes and deepens the insights of the second.

> The young disciple Ratthapala went to King Koravya's Migācīra garden and sat down at the root of a tree for the day's abiding.[1]

This could mean that he intends to meditate, or that he is planning to spend the rest of the day there without anything in particular to do, since such an advanced practitioner is in no need for distraction or busy-work. When news gets out that he is there, the king of the land puts an immediate stop to his afternoon's entertainments and decides to visit the young holy man. He takes his entire court with him—like the CEO of a great company flying to a spiritual retreat in his private jet and bringing with him all his accessories of status and luxury. Ratthapala at once sees that the visit is a demonstration of power, and gently puts the king in his place:

> King Koravya had a number of state carriages prepared, and mounting one of them, accompanied by the other carriages, he drove out from Thullakoṭṭhita with the full pomp

---

[1] Bhikkhu Bodhi (trans.), "On Ratthapala," *Majjhima Nikaya 82*, SuttaCentral. https://suttacentral.net/en/mn82.

of royalty to see the venerable Raṭṭhapāla. He drove thus as far as the road was passable for carriages, and then he dismounted from his carriage and went forward on foot with a following of the most eminent officials to where the venerable Raṭṭhapāla was. He exchanged greetings with the venerable Raṭṭhapāla, and when this courteous and amiable talk was finished, he stood at one side and said:

"Here is an elephant rug. Let Master Raṭṭhapāla be seated on it."

"There is no need, great king. Sit down. I am sitting on my own mat."

As anyone who has had dealings with strong-willed successful people will instantly recognize, the king's offer of a luxury rug is not in fact a courtesy, but an imposition masquerading as a courtesy—an attempt to start the discussion on his own terms and to have Ratthapala demonstrate to everyone present who the master is here. Ratthapala quietly refuses the offer, orders the king to sit, and suggests that he needs nothing that the king can offer. It turns out that the king does not have a question concerning his own plight, but has come to marvel at the oddity of a healthy young nobleman becoming a mendicant:

"Master Raṭṭhapāla, there are four kinds of loss. Because they have undergone these four kinds of loss, some people here shave off their hair and beard, put on the yellow robe, and go forth from the home life into homelessness. What are the four? They are loss through aging, loss through sickness, loss of wealth, and loss of relatives...What has he known or seen or heard that he has gone forth from the home life into homelessness?"

In a society where it is customary only for those who are close to the end of their lives to renounce everything and take to wandering, this is a reasonable question. Why else would a sane person to choose to be homeless? It is a natural choice in the face of losing everything that is dear to one—the ability to live and function for oneself and others, health, financial means, and close relationships, including friends. When these are all gone, then it makes sense to cast oneself out onto the mercy of the world; but when strength, health, wealth, and love are all still available, it makes no sense at all.

Ratthapala's answer is simple and profound, the essence of what he has learned from the Buddha:

> "Great king, there are four summaries of the Dhamma that have been taught by the Blessed One who knows and sees, accomplished and fully enlightened. Knowing and seeing and hearing them, I went forth from the home life into homelessness. What are the four?
>
> (1) "'Life in any world is unstable, it is swept away': this is the first summary of the Dhamma taught by the Blessed One who knows and sees, accomplished and fully enlightened. Knowing and seeing and hearing this, I went forth from the home life into homelessness.
>
> (2) "'Life in any world has no shelter and no protector': this is the second summary of the Dhamma taught by the Blessed One who knows and sees...
>
> (3) "'Life in any world has nothing of its own; one has to leave all and pass on': this is the third summary of the Dhamma taught by the Blessed One who knows and sees...
>
> (4) "'Life in any world is incomplete, insatiate, the slave of craving': this is the fourth summary of the Dhamma taught by the Blessed One who knows and sees...'"

It is important both to know and to see—that is, to experience for ourselves. When he explains these teachings in detail, Ratthapala will bring them down to earth by drawing the king's attention to his own life. For example, with the first teaching, after the king has described the almost superhuman physical prowess of his youth --

> "What do you think, great king? Are you now as strong in thighs and arms, as sturdy and as capable in battle?"
>
> "No, Master Raṭṭhapāla. Now I am old, aged, burdened with years, advanced in life, come to the last stage; my years have turned eighty. Sometimes I mean to put my foot here and I put my foot somewhere else."

This is a simple but resonant image for all the effects of aging, not least the perplexing disconnections between desires, thoughts, the body's abilities, and physical location: *Sometimes I mean to put my foot here and I put my foot somewhere else.* When the king realizes the relevance to himself of this first teaching, he becomes enthusiastic about the accurate conciseness of the Buddha's words, which seemed so abstract and general at first:

> "It is wonderful, Master Raṭṭhapāla, it is marvelous how well that has been expressed by the Blessed One who knows and sees, accomplished and fully enlightened: 'Life in any world is unstable, it is swept away.' It is indeed so!"

At eighty, he can feel that the teaching is speaking directly to him. Nonetheless, for a king, how could the second teaching be true?

> "Master Raṭṭhapāla, there exist in this court elephant troops and cavalry and chariot troops and infantry, which will serve to subdue any threats to us. Now Master Raṭṭhapāla said: 'Life in any world has no shelter and no protector.' How should the meaning of that statement be understood?"

We can substitute his terms with the terms that express our own accumulated securities: the mortgage and health insurance, the retirement plans and extra savings, the systems of defense and laws that guarantee our peace. The teacher then unobtrusively shifts the terms of the question away from material protections and towards a different kind of vulnerability:

> "What do you think, great king? Do you have any chronic ailment?"
>
> "I have a chronic wind ailment, Master Raṭṭhapāla. Sometimes my friends and companions, kinsmen and relatives, stand around me, thinking: 'Now King Koravya is about to die, now King Koravya is about to die!'"
>
> "What do you think, great king? Can you command your friends and companions, your kinsmen and relatives: 'Come, my good friends and companions, my kinsmen and relatives. All of you present share this painful feeling so that I may feel less pain'? Or do you have to feel that pain yourself alone?"
>
> "I cannot command my friends and companions, my kinsmen and relatives thus, Master Raṭṭhapāla. I have to feel that pain alone."

At this point in the dialogue Ratthapala forces the king to confront the disagreeable but fundamental fact of our solitude: no one can fully understand what it is like to be us, no one can really feel our joys and sorrows with us, no one can participate in our experience and by so doing dilute our pain. What we suffer, we suffer alone—and no other person, not even in a small way, can live our lives for us. In our day to day social interactions it is easy to distract ourselves with the sweet balm of company, but in life's profound crises we always know that we are alone—not physically, not socially, but alone in our experiencing. Other religions answer the aloneness with God, in prayers or in Psalms, but in the world of the Buddha there is no transcendent solution to solitude. This may be one of the toughest sticking-points in the Buddha's vision of life; most of us yearn so intensely for companionship, either of friends or of lovers or of a divine being, that a philosophical starting-point of utter aloneness seems impossibly bleak and repellent. How could our yearning for companionship be nothing more than craving after an illusion? It takes an unusually strong spirit to be able to swallow this and continue the work, or a spirit that sees with absolute clarity that the alternatives lead nowhere.

After reminding the king of aging and solitude, Ratthapala then ties both threads together into an account of ineluctable dispossession, in which everything we have is left behind as we find ourselves impelled onwards in the rushing river made up of the antecedents and consequences of actions.

> "What do you think, great king? You now enjoy yourself provided and endowed with the five cords of sensual pleasure, but will you be able to have it of the life to come: 'Let me likewise enjoy myself provided and endowed with these same five cords of sensual pleasure'? Or will others take over this property, while you will have to pass on according to your actions?"
>
> "I cannot have it thus of the life to come, Master Raṭṭhapāla. On the contrary, others will take over this property while I shall have to pass on according to my actions."

On a physical level, this seems obvious: when we die, we have to say goodbye to everything and everyone, and nothing that we held to be "ours" can come with us. But this "everything" includes the contents of our consciousness, our perceptions, and our feelings; even these are not things that we can "possess" and take with us. Indeed, even the sense of "us" does not persist down this raging river.

What is left to us then but this present moment? Can we not be satisfied with what we have in the Now? Ratthapala engages this with a simple practical question, which the king to his credit answers honestly:

> "Now Master Raṭṭhapāla said: 'Life in any world is incomplete, insatiate, the slave of craving.' How should the meaning of that statement be understood?"
>
> "What do you think, great king? Do you reign over the rich Kuru country?"
>
> "Yes, Master Raṭṭhapāla, I do."
>
> "What do you think, great king? Suppose a trustworthy and reliable man came to you from the east and said: 'Please know, great king, that I have come from the east, and there I saw a large country, powerful and rich, very populous and crowded with people. There are plenty of elephant troops there, plenty of cavalry, chariot troops and infantry; there is plenty of ivory there, and plenty of gold coins and bullion both unworked and worked, and plenty of women for wives. With your present forces you can conquer it. Conquer it then, great king.' What would you do?"
>
> "We would conquer it and reign over it, Master Raṭṭhapāla."

The exchange is repeated verbatim with regard to the other three directions: even the king of the Kurus, who has everything we can imagine having and more, is not satisfied with his magnificent lot—and he admits it.

> "Great king, it was on account of this that the Blessed One who knows and sees, accomplished and fully enlightened, said: 'Life in any world is incomplete, insatiate, the slave of craving'; and when I knew and saw and heard this, I went forth from the home life into homelessness."

Reading this, it is tempting for an ordinary person to wonder if only power-hungry egomaniacs are susceptible to this state of constant insatiability, but Ratthapala wants us to look into our own hearts and see for ourselves. For instance, I enjoy the variety of food I eat and have no shortage both of nutrition and of taste—but I am nonetheless always interested in new recipes and fascinated by new foods. I have hundreds of books at home and on my e-reader, and of those there may be a hundred I haven't yet read staring me in the face every day—yet if I were to browse the shelves of a bookshop or scroll through the bargains on Amazon, I will almost certainly be adding at least one more book to my collection. The insatiability extends to far more than physical possessions, and a few minutes of self-examination will show that with our thoughts and experiences, our hobbies and employments, our friendships and romantic involvements, it is very hard to accept that we have enough. I know the dictionary definition of *enough*, but it is evident that I haven't understood the meaning of the word. We each seem to have a hole in our heart that nothing is big enough to fill. To many religions, such a thought would be a tragic heresy—how could it be true that we have a yearning that cannot be satisfied? Or is this yearning infinite, such that it can be satisfied only by an infinite being? The infinite being therefore has to exist, otherwise we are doomed to ceaseless agitation and despair. However, Ratthapala spurns this consolation; he has recognized and accepted the truth of insatiable craving as a basic condition of life, just as aging, flux, and solitude are. "Yearning for the infinite" is only a pretty euphemism for the suffering that comes from craving, and, seeing clearly that life is an agitation that cannot be stilled, he will have none of it.

King Koravya is obviously impressed by the young man's austere strength of mind and mastery of desire; a powerful king can respect such nobility of aspiration and unbending resolve. Ratthapala, on the other hand, does not present the king with difficult teachings about the nature of the soul and dependent origination, but instead gives him four handles that he can easily grasp—and that open doors to some very deep insights if the king should choose to contemplate them further. Ratthapala's claim is not that these insights are the whole of the Buddha's teaching, but that they are summaries, sketches, that need to be fleshed out and filled in by reflection on our own experience. They encapsulate our condition, and if we understand this condition we will find ourselves no longer able to stomach the normal run of things and unwilling to continue slowly drowning in the sea of dissatisfaction. He seems to have understood all of this the first time he heard the Buddha, as a mere boy. What kind of person is this, who can hear so deeply the first time?

To answer this we have to turn to the first half of the sutta, which describes in bleak comic detail Ratthapala's great battle against temptation.

26. The Great Teenage Refusal: A Buddhist Comedy
Ratthapala, Pt.2

Who is this Ratthapala who cannot be intimidated by a mighty king and who sets this king a new standard of strength and mastery?

He is introduced as a scion of a wealthy Brahmin family from the once great kingdom of the Kurus, at the foot of the Himalayas. When the Buddha wanders into town, Ratthapala accompanies the other brahmin householders to hear this famous guru teach and is at once so moved by the teaching that he asks the Buddha if he can leave everything and join him. The Buddha replies: *"Raṭṭhapāla, Tathāgatas do not give the going forth to anyone who does not have his parents' permission."* This might be read as disingenuous, since the Buddha himself simply left his family without anyone's permission—but he is probably telling this to Ratthapala because he knows that youthful impetuousness and shallow zeal are best tested by parental disapproval and obstruction.

The young man's reply is evidence of a strong-willed child used to getting his way with his parents: *"Venerable sir, I shall see to it that my parents permit me to go forth from the home life into homelessness."* When he asks his parents he is told, predictably,

> "Raṭṭhapāla, you are our only son, dear and beloved. You have been raised in comfort, brought up in comfort; you know nothing of suffering, dear Raṭṭhapāla. Even in case of your death we would lose you unwillingly, so how could we give you our permission to go forth from the home life into homelessness while you are still living?"

To Ratthapala, this appeal is impotent because he despises the way his family lives and cannot imagine any satisfaction for himself from their coarse materialistic existence. To his parents, he is being typically willful and impulsive, and needs to see that they are acting only out of love for him and care for his best interests. Of course these parents do not understand the Buddha's teachings; to them, the guru provided interesting entertainment with some instruction, but did not inspire them with a wish to emulate. Besides, how could any parent envision with equanimity their child living as a homeless person, begging for food and sleeping on the ground wherever he can?—especially a boy brought up with silver spoons and beds of roses. The exchange between them is repeated three times, as if to enact in prose the repetitive intransigence between mutually uncomprehending family members. The conflict has no middle ground and therefore no satisfactory solution for both sides.

> Then, not receiving his parents' permission to go forth, the clansman Raṭṭhapāla lay down there on the bare floor, saying: "Right here I shall either die or receive the going forth."

Taken out of context this reaction looks like a tantrum, but taken in the context of many years spent living with these people Ratthapala's action is an expression of desperation. We have all been in a situation when we know with every cell in our being that if we continue the life we have been living our souls will wither and die, and when we see a path out of this horrible living-death we are only too happy to cast off everything that we have known and are used to. "I have to go, or I am going to die here." The usual effect on those around us is consternation. Something in them must recognize some truth in our reaction, and this provokes a more vehement counter-action against the rejection of their cherished way of life. There is a redoubled effort to win the boy back to the attractions of comfort and pleasure:

> Then the clansman Raṭṭhapāla's parents said to him: "Dear Raṭṭhapāla, you are our only son, dear and beloved. You have been raised in comfort, brought up in comfort; you know nothing of suffering, dear Raṭṭhapāla. Get up, dear Raṭṭhapāla, eat, drink, and amuse yourself. While eating, drinking, and amusing yourself, you can be happy enjoying sensual pleasures and making merit. We do not permit you to go forth from the home life into homelessness. Even in the case of your death we would lose you unwillingly, so how could we give you our permission to go forth from the home life into homelessness while you are still living?"

And making merit: You can lead a good life and enjoy yourself, Ratthapala, it doesn't have to be either/or. You don't have to give up all the comforts that a reasonable human being lives for! Ratthapala of course hears this as a soul-killing compromise: "By these I would not care to die, / Half convention and half lie."[1] His family cannot grasp not only that he has no interest whatsoever in comfort, pleasure, amusement, and the accumulation of merit that results in prolonged comfort, pleasure, and amusement—but that he is actually repelled by the sheer meaninglessness of the round of porcine contentment. Most people want nothing more than this: a comfortable life with as few inconveniences and troubles as possible. It takes an intelligent teenager to perceive that even when people have all of this they are still peevish and unhappy, and none of the "good things" of life have any power to make them better or happier. But to them, Ratthapala's refusal is unintelligible, and he knows that nothing he can say will have any persuasive impact. *So, when this was said, the clans-*

---

[1] Dylan Thomas, "I Have Longed to Move Away," *Selected Poems, 1934-1952* (New Directions: 2003) 69.

man Raṭṭhapāla was silent. The exchange is repeated:

> For the second time...For the third time his parents said to
> him: "Dear Raṭṭhapāla...how could we give you our per-
> mission to go forth from the home life into homelessness
> while you are still living?" For the third time the clansman
> Raṭṭhapāla was silent.

They attempt to break the impasse by enlisting his friends,
who reiterate the temptation but see more quickly than the parents do that their friend is obdurate:

> Then the clansman Raṭṭhapāla's friends went to his par-
> ents and said to them: "Mother and father, the clansman
> Raṭṭhapāla is lying down there on the bare floor, having
> said: 'Right here I shall either die or receive the going
> forth.' Now if you do not give him your permission to go
> forth from the home life into homelessness, he will die
> there. But if you give him your permission, you will see him
> after he has gone forth. And if he does not enjoy the going
> forth, what else can he do then but return here? So give
> him your permission to go forth from the home life into
> homelessness."
> "Then, dears, we give the clansman Raṭṭhapāla permis-
> sion to go forth from the home life into homelessness. But
> when he has gone forth, he must visit his parents."

This seems to be an entirely sensible solution; after all, most
young people smitten with spiritual ideals are quite likely to give
up after some experience of the difficulties of living up to them.
Once again, Ratthapala's parents demonstrate that they simply
do not know their child; indeed, this may itself be a significant
reason for his anger at them—that they are so blinded by the life
of material luxury that they are unable to see the unhappiness of
the individuals closest to them.

Against their hopes and expectations, Ratthapala blossoms under spiritual cultivation. He is a "natural:"

> Before long, dwelling alone, withdrawn, diligent, ardent, and resolute, the venerable Raṭṭhapāla, by realising for himself with direct knowledge, here and now entered upon and abided in that supreme goal of the holy life for the sake of which clansmen rightly go forth from the home life into homelessness. He directly knew: "Birth is destroyed, the holy life has been lived, what had to be done has been done, there is no more coming to any state of being." And the venerable Raṭṭhapāla became one of the arahants.

At this point he asks the Buddha if he can visit his parents, and the Buddha, seeing that the young arahant has passed beyond all susceptibility to familial seduction, says yes. Now why does Ratthapala want to go back? Is it solely because he has promised to do so, and a noble spirit will keep his vows? If so, it must be a task that he will now discharge with cold efficiency and some distaste. Or is it as many of us have experienced going home after many years away in a new life: we have to return just once, to verify for ourselves that the old life was exactly as oppressive as we remember it to have been, and that we have indeed freed ourselves for good as well as for the good of all?

> Now on that occasion the venerable Raṭṭhapāla's father was sitting in the hall of the central door having his hair dressed. When he saw the venerable Raṭṭhapāla coming in the distance, he said: "Our only son, dear and beloved, was made to go forth by these bald-pated recluses." Then at his own father's house the venerable Raṭṭhapāla received neither alms nor a polite refusal; instead, he received only abuse.

The detail of his father sitting in the hall of the central door having his hair dressed is a wonderful image of the life of indolent and ostentatious luxury, and in the bosom of this life, once again, he fails to recognize his son. It takes a maid from whom Ratthapala begs cold leftover porridge to recognize him, and now the mortified father comes running out:

> Just then the venerable Raṭṭhapāla was eating the old porridge by the wall of a certain shelter. His father went to him and said: "Raṭṭhapāla, my dear, surely there is...and you will be eating old porridge! Is there not your own house to go to?"
> "How could we have a house, householder, when we have gone forth from the home life into homelessness? We are homeless, householder. We went to your house, but we received neither alms nor a polite refusal there; instead we received only abuse."
> "Come, dear Raṭṭhapāla, let us go to the house."
> "Enough, householder, my meal for today is finished."

In other words: I don't need you and don't want you. Ratthapala's coldness of speech verges on aggression; the word "householder" functions as a high barbed wire fence, which not only keeps intruders out but looks so bristly that they won't even think of coming in. Shouldn't Ratthapala have been softer, friendlier, to his dear father who cannot help loving him in the only way he knows how? Why does he have to be so harsh, since the harshness in this case can deliver only wounds but no comprehension? When a young person insists on eating leftover porridge on the street while his father pleads with him in vain to come home and have a decent meal, he obviously intends to upset, humiliate, and cause pain. While the Buddha knows that there is no possibility of Ratthapala's reversion to the old life, he must also see that the young arahant needs to return home one more time to make the definite violent cut—in this case by forcefully putting his father in his place and demonstrating, for himself as well as his father, that the filial relationship no longer exists.

Later that day, when Ratthapala reluctantly goes to a feast arranged for him by his father, he is shown two heaps of gold and told that they are all his, to be used in a life that any mortal would envy. Instead of polite refusal, he rejects it all with contempt:

> "Householder, if you would follow my advice, then have this pile of gold coins and bullion loaded on carts and carried away to be dumped midstream in the river Ganges. Why is that? Because, householder, on account of this there will arise for you sorrow, lamentation, pain, grief, and despair."

—as if his father were capable of understanding this admonition!

> Then the venerable Ratthapāla's former wives clasped his feet and said to him: "What are they like, my lord's son, the nymphs for whose sake you lead the holy life?"
> "We do not lead the holy life for the sake of nymphs, sisters."
> "Our lord's son Ratthapāla calls us 'sisters,'" they cried and right there they fainted.

Every conceivable attempt is made to win him back to the life of comfort, until Ratthapala cuts it short with a comically cruel command:

> "Householder, if there is a meal to be given, then give it. Do not harass us."
> "Eat then, dear Ratthapāla, the meal is ready."
> Then, with his own hands, the venerable Ratthapāla's father served and satisfied him with the various kinds of good food.

192

From the point of view of most Asian traditions, the inversion of filiality in the image of the aged father serving the renegade son would be both touching and shocking. Moreover, the son lets himself be served by his father, and eats without pleasure or gratitude; the drama is simultaneously perverse, unnatural, and cruel. The father has been reduced to silence, and he must know that this will be his last opportunity to serve his own son at home. *Then, with his own hands, the venerable Raṭṭhapāla's father served and satisfied him with the various kinds of good food.* The meal has now turned into a sacred valediction, ritually and tenderly—*with his own hands*—administered by the father.

Is Ratthapala at all moved by this?

When the venerable Raṭṭhapāla had eaten and had put his bowl aside, he stood up and uttered these stanzas:

"Behold a puppet here pranked out,
A body built up out of sores,
Sick, an object for concern,
Where no stability abides.

Behold a figure here pranked out
With jewellery and earrings too,
A skeleton wrapped up in skin,
Made attractive by its clothes.

Its feet adorned with henna dye
And powder smeared upon its face:
It may beguile a fool, but not
A seeker of the further shore.

Its hair is dressed in eightfold plaits

And unguent smeared upon its eyes:
It may beguile a fool, but not
A seeker of the further shore.

A filthy body well adorned
Like a new-painted unguent pot:
It may beguile a fool, but not
A seeker of the further shore.

The deer-hunter set out the snare
But the deer did not spring the trap;
We ate the bait and now depart
Leaving the hunters to lament."

The stanzas are an expression of disgust and triumph, with some element of cold rage; they feel like a parting curse. There is no way that the king could understand why his son is saying these things, and Ratthapala must know that. Thus the stanzas are intended to inflict a painful rejection, as well as to fortify a final relinquishing of the old life: Nice try, but you failed to trap me. What Ratthapala fails to see is the ambivalence of his father's attempt: yes, it was a trap, but not merely a trap; the father is trying to love in the way that he knows how. It may be that love of this kind is really nothing more than a trap, a device to possess and control—but what would it take for a person to notice this confusion in himself? If he errs, it is more from ignorance than from malice, and what he needs is to be instructed. Ratthapala also doesn't see the ambivalence of his own reaction: yes, the noble soul has succeeded in holding out against the seductions of pleasure and the soft life of mortals who have no higher aspirations, but the vexed haughtiness of the noble soul betrays a certain neediness—for what? For understanding and respect? A helpless and unreasonable demand that those closest to him be better and wiser than they are? Why can't his family just be like him? The accusation of the parting stanzas barely conceals a raging disappointment in the failings of ordinary people.

At this point Ratthapala leaves his father's house and settles down for the day in King Koravya's Megacira Garden—either completely satisfied that he now no longer needs to think of his family again, or to still his furious, grieving heart. The arahant who asserts his mastery in instructing the king has revealed himself to us as a young man of iron will and truculent pride—not a humane, compassionate Buddha or one with skill in saying to people what they need to hear. His summaries of the Buddha's teachings express the vision of a fierce but rigid spirit, one who bends to no one, and who lets it be known that he bends to no one. Perhaps it takes such a character to command the attention of the Kuru king.

27. Je Suis Ajatasattu:
Tragedy of the Samaññaphala Sutta (1)

"History, Stephen said, is a nightmare from which I am trying to awake." —Joyce, *Ulysses*

History can seem nothing more than a dismal recitation of greed, theft, lust, machinations, murder, usurpation, and violent conquest. Our newspapers intone a daily version of this record, softened with entertainment and sports. If an extraterrestrial being were to study a library full of histories and newspapers, he would be entirely justified in wishing for the extermination of a species so stupid and destructive. Our literary and spiritual traditions stand as consolations against the bleak self-portrait painted by our collective deeds: we know that every history book and newspaper depicts us as a toxic, tumultuous species, but surely that can't be all we are? In every great civilization there are attempts to end the cycle of misery, sometimes by re-conceiving the structure of societies, sometimes by the actual political attempt to force a new order—but mostly by re-envisioning human possibilities and acculturating a new kind of person, one who has the wisdom to understand the deadly old cycle and the will to transcend it. Plato conceives The Philosopher; the authors of the Bible give us various versions of followers of God; Confucius has the *junzi* or superior person; the Daoist writers describe the freely wandering sage; while in the Hindu schools different versions of the liberated spirit can be found bickering with one another. In the Pali Canon we encounter not only the new kind of being called the Buddha or *Tathagata*, as perplexing and revolutionary then as now, but also the bhikkhu or wandering mendicant, an aspiring Buddha. The bhikkhu came from all walks of

life, all castes, and could be old or young. Hundreds of them
would accompany the Buddha in his wandering, and probably
hundreds more would be engaged in solitary meditation beyond
the walls of civilized life. In a system where the renunciation of
society was reserved for the very old, those who were "done" with
their lives and on their way out, the vigorous and determined
bhikkhu would have seemed a puzzling phenomenon, one that
required explanation. What good is such a person, and why
would anyone choose to live as a homeless beggar when more
peasant options were available? What could he possibly be thinking?

The *Digha Nikaya* or *Longer Discourses of the Buddha* begins
with a substantial sutta, the *Brahmajala*, that has been subtitled
"What the teaching is not." It is followed by a sutta that gives an
overview of the entire Buddhist path, but this overview—which
occurs almost verbatim in several other suttas—comes embedded
in a moving and profound narrative that is also one of the literary
masterpieces of the Pali Canon. The *Samannaphala Sutta*, sometimes called "The Fruits of the Homeless Life," begins like this:

> Thus have I heard. On one occasion the Exalted One was
> dwelling at Rājagaha, in Jīvaka Komārabhacca's Mango
> Grove, together with a large company of twelve hundred
> and fifty bhikkhus. At the time, on the fifteenth-day
> Uposatha, the full-moon night of Komudī in the fourth
> month, King Ajātasattu of Magadha, the son of Queen
> Videhā, was sitting on the upper terrace of his palace sur-
> rounded by his ministers.[1]

The phrase "at the time," which can also be translated
"meanwhile," brings to our attention two parallel worlds that are
set to collide. On the one hand there is an unusually large gath-

---

[1] Bhikkhu Bodhi (trans.), "The Fruits of Recluseship," *Digha Nikaya* 2, SuttaCentral. https://suttacentral.net/en/dn2.

ering of bhikkhus around a sage, embodying aspiration for a better life or for total freedom from the old cycles of suffering. On the other, there is the court of the notorious King Ajatasattu, the archetypal ancient monarch, incarnating conquest, ruthless ambition, and terrifying violence: he is the Spirit of the World, the essence of man the historical actor, brutal and unregenerate. As always, he is surrounded by aspiring despots, wealthy enablers, pleasure-slaves, calculating sycophants, and one or two wise counsellors who are trying to "ride the tiger." They all know no difference between night and day because their king, from fear and guilt, cannot sleep.

> There the king uttered the following joyful exclamation:
> "How delightful, friends, is this moonlit night! How beautiful is this moonlit night! How lovely is this moonlit night! How tranquil is this moonlit night! How auspicious is this moonlit night! Is there any recluse or brahmin that we could visit tonight who might be able to bring peace to my mind?"

Even in his insomniac torment, Ajatasattu is capable of rejoicing in the beauty of the moonlight, and rather than submerging himself in pleasurable distractions he wants to spend the night seeking balm for his troubled spirit. This king has not yet drowned in the world, to the point of not noticing his own perturbation; this sets him apart from all those ambitious people who are so used to the World that they cannot even recognize their own unhappiness. Ajatasattu is looking for someone who has found a definitive peace, and after his advisors suggest various gurus in the vicinity he chooses to visit the Buddha—taking with him the entire paraphernalia of his power and prestige, a royal army of thousands. To go as a lone human being would be unthinkable for him; he is no longer able to think of himself apart from his vast retinue, and is perhaps afraid to do so.

King Ajātasattu then had five hundred of his women mounted on the female elephants, one on each, while he himself mounted his personal bull-elephant. With his attendants carrying torches, he went forth from Rājagaha in full royal splendour, setting out in the direction of Jīvaka's Mango Grove.

There is a lesson for all of us here. In one of Zhuangzi's parables, a budding spiritual seeker is refused entry to the house of a sage because the sage is willing to see him but not the "whole crowd of people he has brought with him." What is meant here is the multitude of people and things necessary to maintain our lives, positions, earthly comforts, and egos: all the enablers and sustainers of material security, but also the inner voices, of old friends and enemies, books, teachers, the formative mental influences. We bring a noisy crowd with us wherever we go. Ajatasattu's support system is physically huge, but no huger than our own; his is just more explicit. As long as a person refuses to remove himself from the outsized apparatus that guarantees the world he lives in, will he be able to hear words that "bring peace to the mind"? Just imagine the tramping hubbub of 500 elephants in the night, together with the clamor of all those people talking and of their boots on the road.

Surprisingly, even with such an army at his back, Ajatassatu takes fright on approaching the bhikkhus:

When King Ajātasattu was not far from the Mango Grove, he was suddenly gripped by fear, trepidation, and terror. Frightened, agitated, and terror-stricken, he said to Jīvaka: "You aren't deceiving me, are you, friend Jīvaka? You aren't betraying me? You aren't about to turn me over to my enemies? How could there be such a large company of bhik-khus, twelve hundred and fifty bhikkhus, without any sound of sneezing or coughing, or any noise at all?"

It is wondrously strange that silence can terrify more than noise. The deliberate, coordinated discipline expressed in the bhikkhus' silence strikes him as ominous, like the silence before an ambush—but perhaps this is the only silence he knows. Beyond this, the silence feels unnatural, even monstrous; his terror is an amplified version of a normal person's inability to experience pure silence and his need to fill it up with music, talk, and internal noise. At least the ceaseless babble is in some way predictable, whereas out of silence anything may come.

After his physician reassures him that nothing is amiss,

> King Ajātasattu then approached the Exalted One and stood to one side. As he stood there surveying the company of bhikkhus, which sat in complete silence as serene as a calm lake, he uttered the following joyful exclamation: "May my son, the Prince Udāyibhadda, enjoy such peace as the company of bhikkhus now enjoys!"
>
> [The Exalted One said:] Do your thoughts, great king, follow the call of your affection?"
>
> "Venerable sir, I love my son, the Prince Udāyibhadda. May he enjoy such peace as the company of bhikkhus now enjoys."

Ajatasattu's exclamation appears to be a spontaneous blurt, as if proximity to the Buddha has relaxed his inhibitions and he realizes that he is free to voice what is in his heart. It may be the key to his redemption that his first thought is a thought of love, a thought of another person's benefit; it is also acknowledgment that his son Udayibhaddha is not at peace and needs help. If the blurt indicates what is really on his mind, the question that he officially poses to the Buddha—and that becomes the dominant question for the rest of this sutta—seems only tangentially related to it:

> "There are, venerable sir, various crafts, such as elephant trainers, horse trainers, charioteers, archers, standard bearers, camp marshals, commandos, high royal officers, frontline soldiers, bull-warriors, military heroes, mail-clad warriors, domestic slaves, confectioners, barbers, bath attendants, cooks, garland-makers, laundrymen, weavers, basketmakers, potters, statisticians, accountants, and various other crafts of a similar nature. All those (who practise these crafts) enjoy here and now the visible fruits of their crafts. They obtain happiness and joy themselves, and they give happiness and joy to their parents, wives and children, and their friends and colleagues. They establish an excellent presentation of gifts to recluses and brahmins—leading to heaven, ripening in happiness, conducing to a heavenly rebirth. Is it possible, venerable sir, to point out any fruit of recluseship that is similarly visible here and now?"

All these normal occupations give obvious benefits of various kinds both to their practitioners and to their society, and also to people like monks and ascetics who depend on alms: but what are the benefits of being a bhikkhu? The question is a sensible one, and is still asked today: what good is a life of meditation, a life that can generate no material benefit to anybody? Such a question is not often asked with a sincere desire to know the answer, but is usually rhetorical, presupposing that the answer is "none or very little" and expressing the asker's opinion that the life of a productive member of society is clearly better. If the question is sincere, however, it means that the asker is not happy with his productive life and is genuinely considering the possibility of a change. What does this question mean for Ajatasattu? Why is he really asking it? The Buddha guesses that the king is neither simply insincere nor simply sincere, and sees that the question is probably both a "test" question that might or might not open the door to more serious inquiry. The king is genuinely interested in whether there is an intelligible alternative to living in the World, because on the face of it he has achieved through force the highest successes of such a life and yet is still discontent. The existence of a body of people who can ignore and even disdain the greatest worldly successes is a powerful challenge to him, but as an insatiable conquerer he wants to be challenged by a worthy foe. This is partly why his approach to the Buddha's camp feels like an army engaging another army.

The Buddha guesses that Ajatasattu has already put this "test" question to other gurus, and instead of giving him a straight answer he responds in kind, "testing" the king. He is interested in what other gurus have said, but like a physician sounding out his patient, he needs to understand what the king has made of these answers. "*Do you remember, great king, ever asking other recluses and brahmins this question?*" The question is cheekily phrased—as if it were likely that the king would claim not to remember ever asking this question! It also signals to the king that the Buddha has grasped his modus operandi.

> "I do remember asking them, venerable sir."
> "If it isn't troublesome for you, please tell us how they answered."
> "It is not troublesome for me, venerable sir, when the Exalted One or anyone like him is present."
> "Then speak, great king."

The account that follows of Ajatasattu's interviews with six contemporary sages reads something like the summary of one person's lifelong spiritual quest, as he engages with the different schools of his day. It is one of the many reminders in the Pali Suttas of just how diverse, conflicting, and argumentatively systematic the philosophies of India were at this time. Ajatasattu's eagerness to explore them and his refusal to accept the doctrines he is presented with tells us a lot about his intelligence and integrity.

The first sage he asks is the amoralist Purana Kassapa, who tells him:

> 'Great king, if one acts or induces others to act, mutilates or induces others to mutilate, tortures or induces others to torture, inflicts sorrow or induces others to inflict sorrow, oppresses or induces others to oppress, intimidates or induces others to intimidate; if one destroys life, takes what is not given, breaks into houses, plunders wealth, commits burglary, ambushes highways, commits adultery, speaks falsehood—one does no evil. If with a razor-edged disk one were to reduce all the living beings on this earth to a single heap and pile of flesh, by doing so there would be no evil or outcome of evil. If one were to go along the south bank of the Ganges killing and inducing others to kill, mutilating and inducing others to mutilate, torturing and inducing others to torture, by doing so there would be no evil or outcome of evil. If one were to go along the north bank of the Ganges giving gifts and inducing others to give gifts, making offerings and inducing others to make offerings, by doing so there would be no merit or outcome of merit. By giving, self-control, restraint, and truthful speech there is no merit or outcome of merit.'

Purana Kassapa misinterprets the question about the fruits of recluseship as really being a plea for absolution: he infers that what the king primarily wants is peace, the stilling of a guilty conscience, and that he has no real interest in an alternative way of life. Therefore he tells him simply that it is impossible to do anything good or evil: actions do not matter at all. The doctrine is dogmatically asserted, without reasons given, and the king sees at once that Purana Kassapa has ignored the question but instead of stubbornly insisting on an answer Ajatasattu politely grunts and leaves:

> "Thus, venerable sir, when I asked Pūraṇa Kassapa about a visible fruit of recluseship, he explained to me [his doctrine of] the inefficacy of action. Venerable sir, just as if one asked about a mango would speak about a breadfruit, or as if one asked about a breadfruit would speak about a mango, in the same way when I asked Pūraṇa Kassapa about a visible fruit of recluseship he explained to me [his doctrine of] the inefficacy of action. Then, venerable sir, I thought to myself: 'One like myself should not think of troubling a recluse or brahmin living in his realm.' So I neither rejoiced in the statement of Pūraṇa Kassapa nor did I reject it. But, though I neither rejoiced in it nor rejected it, I still felt dissatisfied, yet did not utter a word of dissatisfaction. Without accepting his doctrine, without embracing it, I got up from my seat and left."

This pattern of engagement is repeated with the other five sages. Mahali Gosala, the fatalist, announces:

> 'Great king, there is no cause or condition for the defilement of beings; beings are defiled without any cause or condition. There is no cause or condition for the purification of beings; beings are purified without cause or condition. There is no self-determination, no determination by others, no personal determination. There is no power, no energy, no personal strength, no personal fortitude. All sentient beings, all living beings, all creatures, all souls, are helpless, powerless, devoid of energy. Undergoing transformation by destiny, circumstance, and nature, they experience pleasure and pain in the six classes of men.
>
> 'There are fourteen hundred thousand principal modes of origin (for living beings) and six thousand [others] and

six hundred (others). There are five hundred kinds of kamma and five kinds of kamma and three kinds of kamma and full kamma and half-kamma. There are sixty-two pathways, sixty-two sub-aeons, six classes of men, eight stages in the life of man, forty-nine hundred modes of livelihood, forty-nine hundred kinds of wanderers, forty-nine hundred abodes of Nāgas, two thousand faculties, three thousand hells, thirty-six realms of dust, seven spheres of percipient beings, seven spheres of non-percipient beings, seven kinds of jointed plants, seven kinds of gods, seven kinds of human beings, seven kinds of demons, seven great lakes, seven major kinds of knots, seven hundred minor kinds of knots, seven major precipices, seven hundred minor precipices, seven major kinds of dreams, seven hundred minor kinds of dreams, eighty-four hundred thousand great aeons. The foolish and the wise, having roamed and wandered through these, will alike make an end to suffering.

'Though one might think: "By this moral discipline or observance or austerity or holy life I will ripen unripened kamma and eliminate ripened kamma whenever it comes up"—that cannot be. For pleasure and pain are measured out. Saṃsāra's limits are fixed, and they can neither be shortened nor extended. There is no advancing forward and no falling back. Just as, when a ball of string is thrown, it rolls along unwinding until it comes to its end, in the same way, the foolish and the wise roam and wander (for the fixed length of time), after which they make an end to suffering.'

"Thus, venerable sir, when I asked Makkhali Gosāla about a visible fruit of recluseship, he explained to me (his doctrine of) purification through wandering in saṃsāra. Venerable sir, just as if one asked about a mango would speak about a breadfruit, or as if one asked about a breadfruit would speak about a mango, in the same way, when I asked Makkhali Gosāla about a visible fruit of recluseship, he explained to me (his doctrine of) purification through wandering in saṃsāra. Then, venerable sir, I thought to myself: 'One like myself should not think of troubling a recluse or brahmin living in his realm.' So I neither rejoiced in the statement of Makkhali Gosāla nor did I reject it. But, though I neither rejoiced in it nor rejected it, I still felt dissatisfied, yet did not utter a word of dissatisfaction. Without accepting his doctrine, without embracing it, I got up from my seat and left."

In this view too there is no such thing as moral action, because there is no real volition or choice. Everything has been pre-caused by an infinite and infinitely complex chain, and all we can do is endure until we die or until the series of causes and consequences that afflict us are played out. Mahali Gosala is also trying to soothe the king's guilt by eradicating the very possibility of guilt, and once again Ajatassatu departs unsatisfied.

He then seeks out the materialist Ajita Kesakambala, who acknowledges no moral or spiritual verities:

'Great king, there is no giving, no offering, no liberality. There is no fruit or result of good and bad actions. There is no present world, no world beyond, no mother, no father, no beings who have taken rebirth. In the world there are no recluses and brahmins of right attainment and right practice who explain this world and the world beyond on the basis of their own direct knowledge and realization. A person is composed of the four primary elements. When he dies, the earth [in his body] returns to and merges with the [external] body of earth; the water (in his body) returns to and merges with the [external] body of water; the fire [in his body]returns to and merges with the [external] body of fire; the air [in his body] returns to and merges with the [external] body of air. His sense faculties pass over into space. Four men carry the corpse along on a bier. His eulogies are sounded until they reach the charnel ground. His bones turn pigeon-coloured. His meritorious offerings end in ashes. The practice of giving is a doctrine of fools. Those who declare that there is [an afterlife] speak only false, empty prattle. With the breaking up of the body, the foolish and the wise alike are annihilated and utterly perish. They do not exist after death.'

"Thus, venerable sir, when I asked Ajita Kesakambala about a visible fruit of recluseship, he explained to me [his doctrine of] annihilation. Venerable sir, just as if one asked about a mango would speak about a breadfruit, or as if one asked about a breadfruit would speak about a mango, in the same way, when I asked Ajita Kesakambala about a visible fruit of recluseship, he explained to me [his doctrine of] annihilation. Then, venerable sir, I thought to myself: 'One like myself should not think of troubling a recluse or brahmin living in his realm.' So I neither rejoiced in the statement of Ajita Kesakambala nor did I reject it. But though I neither rejoiced in it nor rejected it, I still felt dissatisfied, yet did not utter a word of dissatisfaction. Without accepting his doctrine, without embracing it, I got up from my seat and left."

The same type of materialist reduction is given by the atomist Pakudha Kaccāyana, for whom the only reality is atomic, and all human action nothing more than epiphenomenon and therefore illusion:

"'Great king, there are seven bodies that are unmade, unfashioned, uncreated, without a creator, barren, stable as a mountain peak, standing firm like a pillar. They do not alter, do not change, do not obstruct one another; they are incapable of causing one another either pleasure or pain, or both pleasure and pain. What are the seven? The body of earth, the body of water, the body of fire, the body of air, pleasure, pain, and the soul as the seventh. Among these there is no killer nor one who causes killing; no hearer nor one who causes hearing; no cognizer nor one who causes cognition. If someone were to cut off (another person's) head with a sharp sword, he would not be taking [the other's] life. The sword merely passes through the space between the seven bodies.'

"Thus, venerable sir, when I asked Pakudha Kaccāyana about a visible fruit of recluseship, he answered me in a completely irrelevant way. Venerable sir, just as if one asked about a mango would speak about a breadfruit, or as if one asked about a breadfruit would speak about a mango, in the same way, when I asked Pakudha Kaccāyana about a visible fruit of recluseship, he answered me in a completely irrelevant way. Then, venerable sir, I thought to myself: 'One like myself should not think of troubling a recluse or brahmin living in his realm.' So I neither rejoiced in the statement of Pakudha Kaccāyana nor did I reject it. But though I neither rejoiced in it nor rejected it, I still felt dissatisfied, yet did not utter a word of dissatisfaction. Without accepting his doctrine, without embracing it, I got up from my seat and left."

Once again a guru holds out a theory of the world that would grant a kind of absolution to the king's conscience if only he could believe it—and once again the king departs unsatisfied.

The next two sages do not profess to have a view of the whole of things, in light of which all human action can be seen to be nugatory. Nigaṇṭha Nātaputta, more commonly known as Mahavira, the founder of Jainism, offers not absolution but a form of Stoical self-containment in which equanimity comes from doing no harm:

'Great king, a Nigaṇṭha, a knotless one, is restrained with a fourfold restraint. How so? Herein, great king, a Nigaṇṭha is restrained with regard to all water; he is endowed with the avoidance of all evil; he is cleansed by the avoidance of all evil; he is suffused with the avoidance of all evil. Great king, when a Niganṭha is restrained with this fourfold restraint, he is called a knotless one who is self-perfected, self-controlled, and self-established.'

"Thus, venerable sir, when I asked Niganṭha Nātaputta about a visible fruit of recluseship, he explained to me the fourfold restraint. Venerable sir, just as if one asked about a mango would speak about a breadfruit, or as if one asked about a breadfruit would speak about a mango, in the same way, when I asked Niganṭha Nātaputta about a visible fruit of recluseship, he explained to me the fourfold restraint. Then, venerable sir, I thought to myself: 'One like myself should not think of troubling a recluse or brahmin living in his realm.' So I neither rejoiced in the statement of Niganṭha Nātaputta, nor did I reject it. But though I neither rejoiced in it nor rejected it, I still felt dissatisfied, yet did not utter a word of dissatisfaction. Without accepting his doctrine, without embracing it, I got up from my seat and left."

Like the others, he does not answer the question; but unlike the others he does not simply assert a doctrine that makes human action insignificant, and offers something like a path to improvement. But a life consisting of restraint has no appeal for someone like Ajatasattu, and the Nigantha has only replied with negatives and not with any positive benefits to recluseship.

Finally the king discovers the agnostic Sañjaya Belaṭṭhaputta, who abstains from opinions:

'If you ask me:

"Is there a world beyond?" If I thought that there is a world beyond, I would declare to you "There is a world beyond." But I do not say "It is this way," nor "It is that way," nor "It is otherwise." I do not say "It is not so," nor do I say

"It is not not so."

'Similarly, you might ask me the following questions:
"Is there no world beyond?"
"Is it that there both is and is not a world beyond?"
"Is it that there neither is nor is not a world beyond?"
"Are there beings who have taken rebirth?"
"Are there no beings who have taken rebirth?"
"Is it that there both are and are not beings who have taken rebirth?"
"Is it that there neither are nor are not beings who have taken rebirth?"
"Is there fruit and result of good and bad actions?"
"Is there no fruit and result of good and bad actions?"
"Is it that there both are and are not fruit and result of good and bad actions?"
"Is it that there neither are nor are not fruit and result of good and bad actions?"
"Does the Tathāgata exist after death?"
"Does the Tathāgata not exist after death?"
"Does the Tathāgata both exist and not exist after death?"
"Does the Tathāgata neither exist nor not exist after death?"

'If I thought that it was so, I would declare to you "It is so." But do I not say "It is this way," nor "It is that way," nor "It is otherwise." I do not say "It is not so," nor do I say "It is not not so."'

"Thus, venerable sir, when I asked Sañjaya Belaṭṭhaputta about a visible fruit of recluseship, he answered me evasively. Venerable sir, just as if one asked about a mango would speak about a breadfruit, or as if one asked about a breadfruit would speak about a mango, in the same way, when I asked Sañjaya Belaṭṭhaputta about a visible fruit of recluseship, he answered me evasively. Then, venerable sir, I thought to myself: 'One like myself should not think of troubling a recluse or brahmin living in his realm.' So I neither rejoiced in the statement of Sañjaya Belaṭṭhaputta nor did I reject it. But though I neither rejoiced in it nor rejected it, I still felt dissatisfied, yet did not utter a word of dissatisfaction. Without accepting his doctrine, without embracing it, I got up from my seat and left."

In the *Brahmajala Sutta* such evasion is termed "eel-wriggling," and it is impressive that the king sees it for what it is—even though if he had capitulated to this easy agnosticism, it is conceivable that he would have attained a little peace of mind.

Ajatasattu has too much intellectual and moral integrity to be swayed by people who tell him that there is no good or evil, that there is nothing he can be held responsible for, or that his actions do not matter. Some of these doctrines are reminiscent of Krishna's attempts to convince Arjuna in the *Bhagavad Gita* that in destroying the known world he will be doing nothing wrong, and Ajatasattu's unpersuadability is the same as Arjuna's: both know, with every cell of their body, that the arguments—"no one kills, no one is killed"—are specious, ignoble, and impotent. Theories of this sort, so sweeping and so remote from the intensities of the heart, have no power to mollify grief or terror, except in the case of a person who cannot feel deeply. They might help with repressing or numbing unbearable feelings, but Ajatasattu does not want to be numbed. I think he is aware that numbness is also a kind of pain. These six sages offer ways to get him off the hook, but he doesn't want to be let off the hook. As a warrior, he wants to own his deeds and not run away from them or have someone else make them evaporate. The Buddha understands this, and in the description of the homeless life that follows he finds a way to let Ajatasattu reveal and own himself.

If we see Ajatasattu as only an archetype of the ancient sanguinary ruling class, we will have a shallow, disengaged understanding of this Sutta. With his larger-than-life aggressiveness, he is not quite an everyman, but he does embody the unease and anxiety of all thoughtful human beings towards the most fundamental dilemma of our existence. Our desires are insatiable, without limit, and we pursue them, automatically, as far as our abilities and our circumstances let us. This leads to unhappiness, partly because on a deep level we know we cannot be satisfied, and partly because in our efforts to satisfy ourselves we cause harm and destruction, which in turn create guilt and fear: living like this, we cannot be at home in our lives. All of this generates the various dynamisms of history, of samsara. Against this, we want peace, an end to the craving, torment, and agitation—and there is no shortage of teachers who offer different means to peace. Our dilemma is that while we want peace, we also refuse to give up our desires or leave the world created by them. This is exactly the position of Ajatasattu when he comes to the Buddha with all his accoutrements of royal power.

Is there anything the Buddha can say to address the dilemma and resolve it?

28. Tearing Up the Planks:
The Tragedy of Ajatasattu (2)

"I admit the deed! Tear up the planks! Here, here! It is the beating of his hideous heart!" —Poe

Is it possible, venerable sir, to point out any fruit of recluseship that is visible here and now? Ajatasattu's question can be paraphrased: How is the life of a homeless mendicant good for anyone? The phrase visible here and now suggests that he is not interested in present mortification that leads to a better afterlife, whether in heaven or in a subsequent lifetime; nor is he interested in purgatorial affliction that results eventually in final liberation from suffering. He is not a mystic, and is also not attracted by theologies of postponed promise. After all, he takes pride in being a strong man of action who accomplishes his aims with efficient vigor, and who already holds kingdoms in the palm of his hand; he has no need to hope for future goods. His focus is thus entirely on present effects that are evident to the senses. Perceiving this, the Buddha avoids philosophical discussion of the nature of the self or of causation, and concentrates instead on laying out a clear path of practice that can make sense to the king as a better, happier state than the one he enjoys now.

The exposition involves a standard detailed itemization of the the elements of moral discipline, the practices of mindfulness and contentment, the cultivation of higher contemplative states and various forms of wisdom. The same description occurs verbatim in other Suttas, usually in response to a questioner who is asking about the bhikkhu's path; it functions as a memorizable "map" of Buddhist practice, by which we can see where we are and where we need to go, but which also gives reassurances that at any place on the map there are specific tasks and attainments. Other Suttas go into these specific tasks in more detail, but for a practitioner the map is useful as a guide to the whole.

At each stage the Buddha is careful to express what it feels like to accomplish a step on the path. For example,

> "Great king, the bhikkhu who is thus possessed of moral discipline sees no danger anywhere in regard to his restraint by moral discipline. Just as a head-anointed noble warrior who has defeated his enemies sees no danger anywhere from his enemies, so the bhikkhu who is thus possessed of moral discipline sees no danger anywhere in regard to his restraint by moral discipline. Endowed with this noble aggregate of moral discipline, he experiences within himself a blameless happiness."

The bhikkhu is confident of having nothing to fear, either from others or from himself: Endowed with this noble restraint of the sense faculties, he experiences within himself an unblemished happiness. A happiness that is both blameless and unblemished is already far beyond the king's present state of sensual enjoyment, which is shaken and undermined by guilt and anxiety. Nonetheless, the Buddha begins with a portrait of mastery over one's own heart and mind because he knows that the king can imagine this and be moved by it. The point is that what the bhikkhu experiences is *happiness*, not some subtle spiritual state.

The Buddha goes on to say that the bhikkhu is *content*. This word, to modern people who live for stimulation and excitement, seems to be a fairly mild adjective connoting an innocuous, bovine quietude; but in fact what is meant by "contentment" in ancient texts is the powerful self-sufficiency of a truly independent spirit, who craves nothing more than what he already has.

> "And how, great king, is the bhikkhu content? Herein, great king, a bhikkhu is content with robes to protect his body and almsfood to sustain his belly; wherever he goes he

sets out taking only [his requisites] along with him. Just as a bird, wherever it goes, flies with its wings as its only burden, in the same way a bhikkhu is content with robes to protect his body and almsfood to sustain his belly; wherever he goes he sets out taking only [his requisites] along with him. In this way, great king, the bhikkhu is content."

The bhikkhu who has achieved this is free to work without distraction on uprooting all the hindrances to his progress—desires, ill-will and hatred, sloth and torpor, worry, and doubt. When these have been conquered, the bhikkhu will feel the joy of freedom:

"Again, great king, suppose a man were locked up in a prison. After some time he would be released from prison, safe and secure, with no loss of his possessions. He would reflect on this, and as a result he would become glad and experience joy."

"When he sees that these five hindrances have been abandoned within himself, gladness arises. When he is gladdened, rapture arises. When his mind is filled with rapture, his body becomes tranquil; tranquil in body, he experiences happiness; being happy, his mind becomes concentrated."

The Buddha emphasizes *body*: these emotions are felt intensely with one's whole being, and are not merely attenuated spiritual pleasures. He speaks as one who himself has experienced all of this. The various terms for happy feelings—gladness, joy, rapture, tranquility, happiness—are crude attempts to translate words that in Pali denote exact emotional differentiations. Perhaps in English there are far fewer discriminations between forms and stages of happiness.

After working on his character, the bhikkhu is now more receptive to the joys of higher spiritual states (*jhanas*), for each one of which the Buddha gives a beautiful image. For example:

"Great king, suppose a skilled bath attendant or his apprentice were to pour soap-powder into a metal basin, sprinkle it with water, and knead it into a ball, so that the ball of soap-powder be pervaded by moisture, encompassed by moisture, suffused with moisture inside and out, yet would not trickle. In the same way, great king, the bhikkhu drenches, steeps, saturates, and suffuses his body with the rapture and happiness born of seclusion, so that there is no part of his entire body which is not suffused by this rapture and happiness."

"Great king, suppose in a lotus pond there were blue, white, or red lotuses that have been born in the water, grow in the water, and never rise up above the water, but flourish immersed in the water. From their tips to their roots they would be drenched, steeped, saturated, and suffused with cool water, so that there would be no part of those lotuses not suffused with cool water. In the same way, great king, the bhikkhu drenches, steeps, saturates and suffuses his body with the happiness free from rapture, so that there is no part of his entire body which is not suffused by this happiness. This too, great king, is a visible fruit of recluseship more excellent and sublime than the previous ones."

Again, the Buddha emphasizes the body. His path is not one that despises or mortifies the body for the sake of "higher" attainments; indeed, everything we do on this path we do in and with our bodies, and any transformation we experience will also suffuse our bodies. The king has asked for a picture of benefits visible here and now, and the Buddha is assuring him that these benefits are felt powerfully and immediately in every cell and along every vein, like electricity.

The description of the bhikkhu's life culminates in an image of contemplative lucidity. After years of practice, we are able to see ourselves, to look into our lives as we would look into pristine waters:

> "Great king, suppose in a mountain glen there were a lake with clear water, limpid and unsullied. A man with keen sight, standing on the bank, would see oyster-shells, sand and pebbles, and shoals of fish moving about and keeping still. He would think to himself: 'This is a lake with clear water, limpid and unsullied, and there within it are oyster-shells, sand and pebbles, and shoals of fish moving about and keeping still.'
>
> "In the same way, great king, when his mind is thus concentrated, pure and bright .... the bhikkhu directs and inclines it to the knowledge of the destruction of the cankers. He understands as it really is: 'This is suffering' ... He understands: 'Destroyed is birth, the holy life has been lived, what had to be done has been done, there is nothing further beyond this.' This too, great king, is a visible fruit of recluseship more excellent and sublime than the previous ones. And, great king, there is no other fruit of recluseship higher or more sublime than this one."

This is life, this is suffering, this is what it feels like to be done with it all. It is the perspective at the end of medieval epic poems—Boccaccio's *Teseida*, Chaucer's *Troilus* and *Knight's Tale*—when the risen spirit of the dead warrior looks down from the heavens, sees the earth as a winnowing floor, and laughs in his freedom. But how much of this can Ajatasattu possibly understand—he who now is so sunken in inner turmoil that an assembly of silent monks can fill him with terror? To this king who has rejected shortcuts and easy absolutions from other gurus, the Buddha has painted an attractive and convincing path of hard work, with feasible progressions: there is a hope of peace.

Ajatasattu is moved to an exclamation of appreciation and asks to be accepted as a lay-student of the Buddha, as others have done in numerous Suttas—but immediately after this, he makes an extraordinary confession:

> "Venerable sir, a transgression overcame me. I was so foolish, so deluded, so unskilful that for the sake of rulership I took the life of my own father, a righteous man and a righteous king. Let the Exalted One acknowledge my transgression as a transgression for the sake of my restraint in the future."

Why does he suddenly come out with this now? Everyone in his court must already suspect that something like this happened, and know from personal experience that Ajatasattu is capable of a crime of this magnitude, but until the deed rises out of the purblind murk of rumor and finds expression in words, neither the king nor his people can have any closure with the past and no truth on which to build any future thought or action. He needs to come clear. The Buddha's sketch of the path, as it reaches its climactic description of pellucid awareness of one's own life and its true nature, appears to have brought Ajatasattu to a moment in which he is able to perceive himself without obscuration—and then the truth is free to bubble up. It could be that in his previous visits to the other gurus he was looking for someone worthy of hearing the truth, because he already knew that clear utterance would be the beginning of his own freedom; but I think it more probable that his confession is a spontaneous, unpremeditated upsurge of the truth, catalyzed by an encounter with a sage who will not blow him off or lie to him.

> "Indeed, great king, a transgression overcame you. You were so foolish, so deluded, so unskilful that for the sake of rulership you took the life of your father, a righteous man and a righteous king. But since you have seen your trans-

gression as a transgression and make amends for it according to the Dhamma, we acknowledge it. For, great king, this is growth in the discipline of the Noble One: that a person sees his transgression as a transgression, makes amends for it according to the Dhamma, and achieves restraint in the future."

The Buddha's response is sincere, matter of fact, and realistic: the confession is a start, but it has to be backed up with "making amends" and future restraint. It is not in any sense a resolution to anything, since the consequences of past actions—both external and internal—will continue to reverberate, and there is no supernatural power that can annul the causal chains: we live with our actions, and only when we own them is there any hope of working them out. Ajatasattu is obviously an intelligent man with a streak of noble impulse, but his soul is so perturbed by regrets and fears from all his acts of blood that it is hard to imagine that his one glimpse of the light will not quickly be swallowed up again in the vast morass of his inner turmoil and political preoccupations, to exist for him only as a revered memory. His restlessness is so deep and inveterate that he cannot abide in his new state for more than five minutes:

> When this was said, King Ajātasattu said to the Exalted One: "Now, venerable sir, we must go. We have many tasks and duties."
> "Do whatever seems fit, great king."
> Then King Ajātasattu rejoiced in the word of the Exalted One and thanked him for it. Rising from his seat, he paid homage to the Exalted One, circumambulated him, and departed.

Or to paraphrase with modern language: "That was great. Sorry, got to go." While it is true that kings have many heavy duties and urgent tasks, this statement comes too quickly after the confession and sounds like a desire for escape. Moral and spiritual responsibility can be intensely intimidating, and the life of political bustling and jostling will always give welcome refuge and distraction from uncomfortable thoughts. The Buddha's succinct response places responsibility firmly in the king's hands: no one but Ajatasattu himself can decide what he will do next.

Readers of the Suttas see Ajatasattu again at the end of the Buddha's life hatching plans to invade his neighbors, and even though he expresses reverence towards the Buddha it seems that he never again goes to the Buddha or any of his disciples for instruction. Has he given up hope for himself, being able to recognize the greater path but despairing of his ability to walk it? We, and the writers of the discourses, know that he was murdered by his own son, whose peace of mind he cared so much about—perhaps because he feared the patricide that he himself was model for. He knew that in murdering his own father he had crossed over into a hungry realm in which no natural moral inhibition was respected. Moreover, being king and therefore open to the suspicions of everyone, he had dragged his entire kingdom over that invisible line, and now no one was safe and nothing sacred. Ajatasattu's patricide is symbolic of the primal crime in which the political realm is severed from natural morality. Once we find ourselves caught in that cycle—not as victims, but as blind actors—it is very difficult to escape, and the cycle will bite us in the face or in the back. Even if we are lucky enough to get away with our deeds in practical terms, in our hearts we will feel agitations of remorse and anxiety; the cycle gnaws at our innards and eats our sleep.

The Buddha, with clarity and pity, perceives that Ajatasattu cannot attain the peace he seeks:

> Soon after King Ajātasattu had left, the Exalted One addressed the bhikkhus: "This king, bhikkhus, has ruined himself; he has injured himself. Bhikkhus, if this king had

not taken the life of his father, a righteous man and a righteous king, then in this very seat there would have arisen in
him the dust-free, stainless eye of Dhamma."

Or in Maurice Walshe's translation: *"The king is done for, his
fate is sealed..."*[1] There is no way for someone who has murdered
his father for the throne to live a peaceful, happy human life; the
deed itself expresses the character of a person who has already
wandered beyond the pale. Even if that person were capable of
seeing the trouble he is in as well as a path out of it, the past
would hold him with an iron grip and dig iron nails into his
heart. According to an old Vietnamese proverb, you may have
succeeded in reaching the bottom of the mountain safely, but the
rocks you dislodged will continue to hit you in the back for a
while. The danger stops only when all the rocks you have loos-
ened find a resting place.

If there is an afterlife or several afterlives to continue working off crimes and paying off moral debts, there will be hope for
Ajatasattu, and the Buddha's final evaluation implies not in this
life but a subsequent one. But if there is no afterlife, then Ajatasattu's plight is tragic: he is stuck in a cycle that he can recognize
as horrible, and he can see an alternative to the horror—but he is
unable to get unstuck and will die stuck. Thus in midlife he has
given birth in himself to a yearning he will never fulfill. Against
this we might argue that he always has a choice, and can choose
to leave the cycle now and start making amends; he just doesn't
want to, because on a deeper level he loves his vomit and will
always crawl back to it. This kind of choice is only theoretical—
like a drug addict's theoretical ability to quit. The addiction itself
is constituted, among other things, by a multitude of choices,

[1] *"Samannaphala Sutta:* The Fruits of the Homeless Life," *The
Long Discourses of the Buddha,* Maurice Walshe (trans.), (Boston: Wisdom Publications, 1987) 109.

and a single new choice will not counteract the accumulated force of thousands. Read in this way, the discourse might still have some positive lessons: there is a path, it is good and beautiful, we can recognize it as such even from the midst of our mires, and if we understand the suffering of Ajatasattu we will have a better chance of not becoming him. The poetic effect of this discourse is more complex, because Ajatasattu's conversation with the Buddha is in fact a conversation between two sides of our own soul, one lost and one saved. It is both terrible and sublime that the lost soul is still capable of joy and homage when, in its perdition, it meets its saved twin.

A serious student of the Pali Discourses needs to read the collections published by Wisdom Publications. Most of the Suttas quoted in this book can be found in the following beautifully translated volumes:

The Long Discourses of the Buddha: A Translation of the Digha Nikaya. Maurice Walsh, trans. Boston, 1987.

The Connected Discourses of the Buddha: A Translation of the Samyutta Nikaya. Bhikkhu Bodhi, trans. Boston, 2000.

The Middle Length Discourses of the Buddha: A Translation of the Majjhima Nikaya. Bhikkhu Nanamoli, trans. Edited and revised by Bhikkhu Bodhi. 2nd ed. Boston, 2001.

In addition, I have drawn copiously from two websites:

www.accesstoinsight.org
https://suttacentral.net

The former contains almost the entirety of the Pali Discourses in multiple translations, of which I am particularly indebted to the work of Thanissaro Bhikkhu and Soma Thera. The latter is mostly the work of the prodigious Bhikkhu Bodhi, and contains all the Suttas in multiple languages. I thank both Access to Insight and SuttaCentral for their generosity in making these texts freely available to the inquirer.

Access to Insight is also a vast treasure house of commentaries, books, and audio talks on every possible aspect of the Discourses, and it has a valuable subject index. It is possible to download the entire site into one's phone.

Index

Born in Malaysia in 1960 to a South Indian Brahmin father and a Hakka Chinese mother, Krishnan Venkatesh was brought up in England and studied English literature at Magdalene College, Cambridge, where he obtained First Class honors. He subsequently did research for over four years on Shakespeare at the University of Muenster, Germany, as a wissenschaftlicher mitarbeiter for the great Shakespeare scholar Marvin Spevack. From 1986-89 he taught literature and philosophy at Shanxi University, People's Republic of China. Both his personal and academic background make him well suited to being a "bridge" between various traditions. Since 1989 he has taught at St. John's College, Santa Fe, both in the two Western Great Books programs (for which the college is most famous) and was one of the shapers of the unique Eastern Classics Master's program, in which he has taught for over 20 years. The program involves close study of the classics of China, India and Japan, as well as rigorous immersion in Classical Chinese or Sanskrit for the sake of greater intimacy with the texts. Venkatesh has taught in all areas of the program, including Chinese and Sanskrit. From 2003-2008 he was the dean of graduate studies at the college. With Socrates in the Phaedrus, he is skeptical of the value of writing and therefore of publication, and believes strongly in conversation as the most powerful mode of learning – the "writing in the heart." St. John's College has been an ideal academic home for him because of the shared belief in the power of discussion within a sincere community of learning. In the last decade he has spent a total of about two years in India. His recent areas of work have included the Pali Canon of the Buddha, the Japanese philosopher Dogen, and the mathematical books of Johannes Kepler. The lifelong companions at his bedside include Montaigne, Chaucer, Thomas Hardy the poet, Blake, Wordsworth, Zhuangzi, Chekhov, Tolstoy, Austen, Balzac, and Laxness—a beautiful fellowship. Shakespeare is always close at hand.